Responses to
101 Questions
on Death and Eternal Life

Peter C. Phan

PAULIST PRESS
New York / Mahwah, N.J.

This volume is dedicated to the memory of my dad,
who was called to eternal life during the time it was planned
and written,
a reminder that death and eternal life
are not matters to be just talked about
but to be lived daily.

Cover designs for this series are
by James Brisson Design & Production, Williamsville, Vermont

The Publisher gratefully acknowledges use of the following material. Citations of official church documents from Neuner, Josef, S.J., and Dupuis, Jacques, S.J., eds. The Christian Faith in the Doctrinal Documents of the Catholic Church, 6th revised and enlarged edition (New York: Alba House and Bangalore: Theological Publications in India, 1996). Used with permission.

Scripture selections are taken from the New American Bible. Copyright © 1991, 1986, 1970 by the Confraternity of Christian Doctrine, 3211 Fourth Street, N.E., Washington, D.C. 20017-1194 and are used by license of the copyright owner. All rights reserved. No part of the New American Bible may be reproduced in any form without permission in writing from the copyright owner.

Library of Congress Cataloging-in-Publication Data

Phan, Peter C., 1943–
     Responses to 101 questions on death and eternal life / Peter C. Phan.
        p.   cm.
     Includes bibliographical references.
     1. Eschatology—Miscellanea. 2. Death—Religious aspects—Catholic Church—Miscellanea. 3. Future life—Catholic Church—Miscellanea. 4. Catholic Church—Doctrines—Miscellanea. I. Title.
BT821.2.P49   1997
236—dc21   97-19963
                                                                        CIP

Published by Paulist Press
997 Macarthur Boulevard
Mahwah, New Jersey 07430

Printed and bound in the
United States of America

CONTENTS

II. Biblical Eschatology: The End-Time According to the Scriptures

III. Death and Dying: Time Made Eternity

IV. From Death to Resurrection: The Intermediate State

V. Heaven and Hell: With God or Away from God

VII. The Fulfillment of Hope: Back to the Earth

PREFACE

Questions about the afterlife never cease to intrigue, even for people who live in the so-called scientific age. Ironically, it is those who say that there is nothing beyond what is empirically verifiable that keep the issue of the afterlife alive! The afterlife is one of those things that if denied or repressed, will appear elsewhere under another guise. Relentless and, at times, ruthless quests for knowledge, power, fame, money, and pleasure—are they not symptoms of the restlessness of the heart that, to quote Augustine, will not rest until it rests in God?

This perennial interest in the life beyond has recently been boosted by, among other things, near-death experiences, the New Age movement, the threat of nuclear extinction, and, above all, the approaching end of the millennium. Predictions of the coming end of the world, with detailed descriptions of the timetable and events, have become popular again, despite repeated failures of past apocalypticists.

It is my hope that this little book will answer some of the questions frequently asked about death and eternal life. The book is written from the perspective of the Roman Catholic theological tradition, but it is hoped that people of other Christian denominations and non-Christian religions will also find it helpful.

I would like to thank the students in the course on eschatology I taught in the Theological Institute at St. Norbert College, De Pere, Wisconsin, in the summer of 1994. Many of them handed me written questions at the end of the course, and I trust they will find them answered here. I would also like to thank Dr. Howard Ebert, the director of the

1

institute, his wife, Patty, and their two exuberantly energetic daughters, Allison and Jackie, for their many kindnesses. I also owe a debt of gratitude to Kathleen A. Walsh, whose sharp editorial eye has been an invaluable asset. Finally, my deepest gratitude is directed to the Norbertine Fathers of St. Norbert College for their most generous hospitality. Their peace and joy gave me an inkling of what heaven must look like.

INTRODUCTION:
FROM THE PERIPHERY TO THE CENTER:
RECONSTRUCTING ESCHATOLOGY
FOR OUR TIMES

A retrospective glance at the development of Western Christian theology in the last thirty years (from the standpoint of Roman Catholic theology since the conclusion of the Second Vatican Council in 1965) will reveal a dramatic reversal of fortune in the branch of theology called eschatology. Roman Catholics who studied theology in the pre-Vatican II days will remember that eschatology (from the Greek word *eschata,* meaning the last things), the theology of the so-called Last Things—death, judgment, heaven, and hell—was the course they normally took at the end of their theological education.

The central focus of eschatology is the eternal fate of the individual person. Its overriding issue is: What will happen to him or her after death? What captures the attention is not death and dying itself but what follows it. And since what happens after one's death is by nature not verifiable by normal channels of experience and scientific observation, what the prevalent eschatology of those days (which we now call "neo-scholastic") could say on the theme of the afterlife hardly excited the imagination. Even when it did succeed in arousing interest, the concern was usually morbid, and more often than not it bore on irrelevancies, with little implication for the present life and for society in general. The eschatology of that time dealt with a variety of tangential questions, such as what the maximum length of the stay in purgatory would be and how much of it could be reduced by indulgences; how fire in hell, which was held to be material, could burn the soul, which is spiritual; and what kind of worms gnaw at the damned, and how they can survive the heat of hell.

With reason, then, Karl Barth, a Swiss Protestant theologian, called eschatology a harmless tract coming at the end of theology, and Johann Baptist Metz, a German Catholic theologian, described it as a bland treatise promoting empty time and neutralizing the sting of biblical apocalyptic. This does not mean that eschatology could not be and was not wielded as a powerful weapon to scare wayward Christians back to the straight and narrow path of salvation, as evidenced by fire-and-brimstone sermons during retreats and parish missions that harped on the vengeance and wrath of the righteous God against unrepentant sinners.

Since the Second Vatican Council (1962–65), however, radical transformations have taken place in Roman Catholic thought and practice. Eschatology, more than any other branch of theology, may be said to have undergone paradigmatic shifts in both content and methodology. In a nutshell, it moved from the margins to the center of theology. Just as the Copernican revolution dislodged the earth from the center assigned to it by Ptolemaic cosmology and restored the sun to its rightful location, so contemporary eschatology has reshaped all disciplines of Christian theology by reclaiming the position to which it is entitled. Indeed, no Christian doctrine has been left untouched by this directional shift, from the doctrine of God to Christian ethics, with the doctrines of creation, grace, church, and sacraments in between.

From the Periphery to the Center: The Challenge of Culture

Like all currents of thought, contemporary eschatology did not achieve its resurgence in the theological arena in a vacuum. Many factors have contributed to its revitalization as a theological theme. Not all of these factors are theological in nature, nor did they all originate within the walls of the church. Indeed, as faith in search of understanding, or better still, as hope in quest of critical understanding and historical praxis, eschatology received its stimulus for renewal as much from cultural movements as from the *ressourcement* in the Christian Scriptures and Tradition.

Among cultural movements must be included the rise of historical consciousness, the Marxist critique of religion, the growing awareness of the essential unity of the human person, the ecological movement, and the emergence of a sense of existential insecurity. A brief word about each of these and about how they challenge traditional eschatology is in order.

1. It is commonplace to note that with the coming of the Enlightenment in the eighteenth century, a new way of thinking, long in gestation in preceding centuries, emerged in the West; this development is often referred to as the rise of historical consciousness. As Vatican II acknowledged, humankind has substituted "a dynamic and more evolutionary concept of nature for a static one."[1] Whereas classical and medieval philosophies discoursed on eternal, unchangeable, and universal essences, modern thought, aided and abetted by the empirical sciences, views all beings as caught in the web of historical evolution. In particular, there is a clear recognition that human beings are not ready-made and fixed essences. Rather, they are, to use an expression of the German philosopher Martin Heidegger, *"dasein,"* that is, they are *there,* "beings-in-the-world," thrown into time and history as projects pregnant with possibilities and opportunities to be realized in freedom.

This view of humans as ontologically temporal beings calls into question the exclusive focus of traditional eschatology on the beyond and the eternal destiny of the individual, and challenges us to explore the implications of the Christian belief in eternal life for our temporal and worldly responsibilities. Furthermore, if temporality implies "being-toward-death," as Heidegger claims, then death should not be seen merely as a biological event that happens at the end of one's life or merely as the gate through which one passes to enter into eternal life. Rather, death, or more exactly *dying,* can appear as the event throughout one's existence that engages human freedom to the highest degree.

2. Concomitant with the rise of historical consciousness was the critique of religion initiated by Ludwig Feuerbach and carried to its radical conclusion by Karl Marx. For Feuerbach, theology is nothing but anthropology projected to its infinite dimensions. God is humanity writ large. Religion attributes to God qualities that by right belong to humanity and thus alienates human beings from themselves. To counteract this process of self-alienation, Feuerbach recommends that we turn our attention to humanity and its present tasks rather than to God, religion, and otherworldly life.

Whereas for Feuerbach human beings are characterized by consciousness, for Marx we are material and economic beings pure and simple, the product of matter in evolution, spirit being an epiphenomenon of this process. Religion, which is concerned with the spirit and life beyond, is for Marx a soothing distraction from our struggle for economic freedom, especially among the oppressed class. Religion is the opium of the people.

Faced with this critique, the church is impelled to reexamine its eschatological doctrine, especially its understanding of the relationship between social utopias and the kingdom of God, between sociopolitical and economic activities and church activities such as worship and prayer. In particular, such questions are raised as: What is heaven? How is it related to this world? Are justice and peace and economic prosperity part of the kingdom of God? What is the role of the church in the promotion of human well-being? Will human achievements endure? If they do, how?

3. Another nontheological factor that challenges traditional eschatology is the contemporary philosophical understanding of the ontological unity of the human person. Rejected out of hand is any form of dualism in which the human person is viewed simply as a union of body and soul. In light of this anthropology, traditional eschatology, which has not always been free from dualism, is challenged to rethink some of its basic doctrines long taken for granted. For example, can we still say that in death the soul is separated from the body and is unaffected by death? That after death the soul exists apart from the body in a disembodied "intermediate state" between death and the end of the world and waits for a reunion with its body at the resurrection of the dead? That the resurrection implies a getting back of *this* body of ours?

4. The ecological crisis has attracted the attention not only of the scientific community but also of the church.[2] Depletion of the ozone layer, deforestation, the extinction of species, toxic and nuclear waste, the pollution of water and air, global warming, and other forms of environmental destruction pose not only scientific but also ethical and eschatological problems as well.

With regard to eschatology, the ecological crisis raises questions concerning the status of the cosmos in the end-time: What will happen to the cosmos? To the atoms, the sun, the moon, the stars, and billions of galaxies? Will they be destroyed in a universal conflagration? What are the new heaven and the new earth of which the Book of Revelation speaks? Are they a new creation *ex nihilo,* or are they this cosmos transformed?

5. In recent decades there has been in the United States an existential malaise, a pervasive angst about the meaning of life. Whether it is a feeling of satiety caused by overconsumerism, a reaction to yuppie rapaciousness, a fear of extinction by the AIDS epidemic and the ecological disaster, insecurity before the sea changes in the political and economic order, or anxiety at the dawning of a new millennium, this mood has renewed the public interest in death and the afterlife. Recent polls have shown an upsurge among Americans of the belief in angels, reincarnation, the occult, and life beyond death in general. In this *Zeitgeist,* topics that were the standard fare of traditional eschatology and have long been dismissed by modernity as relics of a superstitious era are being taken seriously again.

Neo-Scholastic Eschatology: On the Margins of Theology

In response to these cultural challenges, theologians revisited the neo-scholastic formulation of the doctrine of the end-time and found it woefully inadequate. This eschatology, as taught in seminary theology manuals and familiar to most older Catholics, focused on the fate of the individual: death, individual judgment, purgatory, heaven, hell, resurrection, and beatific vision. There was, no doubt, discussion also of what is called "collective eschatology," for example, the second coming of Christ (the parousia) and the last judgment. However, by and large, neo-scholastic eschatology centered on the *individual's* destiny *after* death. Thus, it acquired a distinctively individualistic and otherworldly cast. The Last Things were seen as objects and events occurring to each individual soul in the world beyond, and the eschatology shaped by this view was rightly characterized by Yves Congar, a French theologian, as "the physics of the beyond."[3]

Methodologically, neo-scholastic eschatology generally made use of the proof-text approach to the Scriptures. The biblical texts were employed not as "source" to generate theological insights but as ornaments to embellish and confirm theories derived from elsewhere. Furthermore, even when it mined the Scriptures and Tradition for insights into the final condition of the individual and society, it tended to take the texts as literal descriptions of the beyond. So theologians expended their mental energies arguing about the nature of fire in purgatory and hell, the possible maximum length of the stay in purgatory, the nature of limbo, the kinds of pains in hell, the characteristics of the risen bodies, and so forth. Historical-critical hermeneutics in its various components did not inform the neo-scholastic approach to Scripture.

Besides narrowing its scope to the eternal destiny of the individual, neo-scholastic eschatology also suffered from a sharp dichotomy between body and soul, the self and the cosmos, the immortality of the soul and the resurrection of the dead, earthly realities and the world beyond, and time and eternity. As a result, a rigid dualism pervaded neo-scholastic eschatology, most often with a depreciation of bodily and earthly realities.

More importantly, because eschatology was literally placed at the end of the study of dogmatic or systematic theology and did not function as the light illuminating other realities of the Christian faith, the theological treatment of these realities obscured their eschatological tension. For example, as the result of this eclipse of eschatology, it was not made clear that the church is the pilgrim people of God on the march toward the *eschaton;* that grace is an anticipation and foretaste of our eternal communion with the Triune God; that all the sacraments, especially the Eucharist, are signs announcing the world to come; and that human beings are oriented toward death.

Conversely, eschatology itself also suffered from this isolation. It could not benefit from the insights derived from the other areas of theology. Again, to give just a few examples, because neo-scholastic eschatology held that the beatific vision, which the blessed enjoy in heaven, is an *immediate* intuition of the divine essence, it was not clear how it is indeed a christological event, mediated by the humanity of Christ. Furthermore, if the beatific vision is a face-to-face seeing of God "clearly, plainly, and openly," as Pope Benedict XII has taught, it was not made plain how it could be reconciled with the doctrine that God is the Incomprehensible Mystery. Nor was it made clear that eternal happiness, as the fulfillment of grace, is essentially a *proper, distinct* communion with each of the divine persons, and not just a generic relation with the divine essence. The role of the Holy Spirit in the resurrection of the dead and in the end-time was not adequately explained. Nor was the connection between faith in the afterlife and ethical commitment to peace and justice made explicit so that the charge that religion is the opium of the people could be convincingly refuted.

Eschatology Back to the Center: Contemporary Movements

The return of eschatology from the margins to the center of theology not only was aided by the "signs of the times" described above but was also provoked by both church events and theological scholarship. Among church events, the Second Vatican Council (1962–65) represented a historical watershed for the Roman Catholic development of eschatology. Not only did the council retrieve the image of the church as a pilgrim people (e.g., *Lumen Gentium,* chap. 7) but also and above all, in its Pastoral Constitution on the Church in the Modern World *(Gaudium et Spes),* it relocated, as it were, heaven back on earth.[4] In this way the council bridged the chasm between the individual and collective eschatology, linked the present with the future, and connected faith with secular activities.

Of course, Vatican II did not drop down all of a sudden from heaven. It was prepared by various movements and people (some of whom were theologians who had been suspected by the Vatican but later rehabilitated). Among theological movements, one should be mentioned in particular, namely, the so-called *Nouvelle Théologie* (with which were associated theologians such as Jean Daniélou, Henri de Lubac—both were made cardinals later—and Henri Bouillard). This movement attempted to overcome the deficiencies of neo-scholastic theology by returning to the sources of the Christian faith *(ressourcement),* in particular, patristic and medieval thinkers. It proposed that eschatology should break away from its individualistic and otherworldly framework and recover its christological, ecclesial, and cosmic dimensions.

Twentieth-century Christian eschatology owed its resurgence to the discovery of the centrality of the kingdom in the preaching and ministry of Jesus. In an ironic twist of history, the failure of nineteenth-century liberal theology's "quest for the historical Jesus" produced one of the most momentous insights for contemporary theology, namely, that apocalypticism and eschatology stood at the center of Jesus' message and ministry and of early Christianity. There ensued a lively debate about whether the kingdom of God in Jesus' preaching was a future reality, a present reality, or both ("consequent," "realized," and "proleptic" eschatologies, respectively).[5] Ernst Käsemann's memorable phrase that "apocalypticism is the mother of all Christian theology,"[6] though obviously a hyperbole, does not miss the mark by much.

This eschatological orientation of Christianity was developed especially by Jürgen Moltmann among Protestant theologians and by Johann Baptist Metz among Roman Catholics.[7] There is no doubt, however, that the theologians who have most profoundly influenced the recent re-envisioning of eschatology are the two theological giants of our century, Karl Rahner and Hans Urs von Balthasar, the former with a more anthropological emphasis, and the latter with a more christological emphasis (not antithesis).[8] Among Orthodox theologians who have contributed significantly to the restoration of eschatology, one could mention the Russian Paul Evdokimov (1900–68).[9]

Eschatology forms the central inspiration for and is a major motif of what can be rightly regarded as the most creative theology of our times, namely, liberation theology. Liberation theology is not a Latin American phenomenon only; it has influenced the way of doing theology in Africa and Asia and has inspired such other theologies as Black and feminist theologies.[10]

In recent times, the Vatican has also paid attention to eschatology. Two documents are of special importance: one, issued by the Congregation for the Doctrine of the Faith in 1979, bearing the title *Recentioris episcoporum sinodi* ("The Reality of Life After Death"); and the other, issued by the International Theological Commission in 1992, titled *De quibusdam quaestionibus actualibus circa eschatologiam* ("Questions in Eschatology").[11] These documents, especially the second one, offer a critique of some contemporary eschatological theories. In particular, they examine the theory of the immediate resurrection in death with the attendant denial of the intermediate state and restate the basic truths of faith regarding the eternal destiny of the individual and history.

Eternal Life: Questions and Answers

In this book, following the question-and-answer format, I will bring up the most frequently asked questions about the afterlife (at least as I have heard them in many discussions about the afterlife) and answer them in a language as free of theological jargon as possible, though some use of the technical language that is part of the Christian Tradition is unavoidable, especially in the first chapter.

Careful readers will be able to distinguish in my answers between what belongs to the truth of the faith and what is a matter of theological speculation, for instance, in the questions about reincarnation, the intermediate state, the nature of the risen body, the millennium, and universal restoration *(apocatastasis)*. This distinction is of special importance in eschatology, given the fact that in many issues in this area the teaching of the church most often concerns the *that* rather than the *how* of things.

It may be useful to state here briefly the basic convictions that undergird both the method and the contents of this book. First of all, one of the most thorny issues in eschatology is the way of approaching the Scriptures (hermeneutics). Anyone with a little familiarity with fundamentalism, of both the Catholic and Protestant varieties, knows that there is no point in discussing whether there will be fire and worms in hell or whether Christ will come down from heaven in the clouds at the end-time (the second coming), amidst the angels' trumpet blasts, to meet his faithful followers in the air ("rapture") and to have them reign with him for a thousand years (the "millennium"), unless one decides *first* how to interpret apocalyptic literature. This does not mean that one will have at the end of the day a certain and universally agreeable interpretation of what the second coming, the rapture, and the millennium mean, but at least one does not waste time asking about the exact date of Christ's parousia (many a self-proclaimed prophet has attempted to foretell the day and hour, and their repeated mistakes did not faze them in the least!), much less about what kind of trumpets the angels will be using and what kind of biological species the hellish worms belong to (yes, there were theologians who raised these questions!).

Given the importance of hermeneutics in eschatology, I have devoted the first chapter to this theme, and I apologize in advance for the unusual length of some of the answers in this chapter (qq. 5–8). The relative difficulty of these answers will be, I hope, clarified when the method is used to answer the questions about the nature of hell and about the manner of the resurrection.

With regard to the contents of the book, I am convinced that one must speak of both individual and collective eschatologies. It is understandable that given past abuses in individual eschatologies, many contemporary theologians (e.g., Hans Küng and Rosemary Radford Ruether) are reluctant to say anything definite about the destiny of the individual and choose to focus almost exclusively on social eschatology. Nevertheless, without pretending to offer a factual description of what will occur to the individual at and after death, it is necessary to present what the Christian faith means to say about it. Thus, it is possible and necessary to present what the Bible, Tradition, and contemporary theology say about, for instance, what happens in death, whether there is a process of purification (purgatory) in or after dying, whether there is an individual judgment, whether there are heaven and hell, whether there is the resurrection of the dead, and so on.

More importantly, to avoid fragmentation in eschatology, the various eschatological realities must be based on Christology; that is, there must be a thoroughgoing "christologization" of eschatology. Whatever we know about eschatology, we know in and through what happens to Jesus in his death and resurrection. The risen Christ is both the cause and model of our afterlife. Eschatology is Christology conjugated in the future tense. The centrality of Christ is manifested not only (though supremely) in the resurrection of the dead but also in the issue of beatific vision and the final fulfillment of human history and the cosmos.

In addition, it is impossible to speak about the end of time today without locating oneself in the context of the scientific discussion of evolution and the end of the cosmos. There has been much discussion in scientific circles of the beginning of time. A new way of looking at the universe called the "common creation story" is emerging. This story emphasizes the one and common origin of all things, including humanity, in the one millionth of a gram of matter from which hundreds of billions of incredibly diverse galaxies, each with billions of stars and planets, have evolved. This new organic model, as opposed to the classic and mechanistic models, emphasizes interrelationships and interdependencies among all beings, living and nonliving, in their similarities as well as differences. There is also the speculation of whether the universe, which began with the Big Bang, will go on forever or will slow down, come to a standstill, and turn into a contraction that will end with another big bang, called the Big Crunch, or will simply die out, without a contraction, when in the last stages of cosmic development the sun goes out and the matter of the stars turns into "ashes."

While clearly recognizing the radical difference between scientific language and the language of faith, it is necessary to recognize and develop one important implication of this common creation story for theological anthropology and eschatology. This new anthropology focuses on the place of human beings as bodies in the universe. It rejects a purely instrumental view of the universe as a resource to be exploited to serve the needs of human beings. The new scientific vision of the universe also demands that, in its presentation of the end-time, Christian eschatology take into account the relationship between the destiny of humanity and that of the material universe. The transworldly view of the physical environment as a temporary abode, a sort of roadside motel, for human beings in their pilgrimage from history to eternity is to be rejected. Rather, the universe and the environment are seen as our home, our permanent address, which shelters us, with which we are in solidarity, and for which we must care.[12]

Lastly, I have attempted to show the intimate connection between faith in the afterlife and commitment to the world, between hope for heaven and labor for peace and justice, between belief in the new heaven and earth and our reponsibilities for the ecology, between contemplation of God and effective love of God's children, especially for the least brothers and sisters of Christ. If we can develop correctly the mutual implications between human freedom and the destiny of human history, between the church and the world, between spirituality and commitment to peace, justice, and responsibilities for the ecology, and above all, if we live these connections in our lives, then Karl Marx's accusation that religion is the opium of the people will prove to be nothing more than a trumped-up charge.

NOTES

[1]*Gaudium et Spes,* no. 5.

[2]See Peter C. Phan, "Pope John Paul II and the Ecological Crisis," *Irish Theological Quarterly* 60, no. 1 (1994): 59–69.

[3]"Bulletin de Théologie Dogmatique," *Revue des Sciences Philosophiques et Théologiques* 33 (1949): 463.

[4]On Vatican II's eschatology, see Carl Peter, "The Last Things and *Lumen Gentium,*" *Chicago Studies* 24 (1985): 225–37.

[5]For a presentation of nine models of eschatology, see Peter C. Phan, *Eternity in Time: A Study of Karl Rahner's Eschatology* (Selinsgrove: Susquehanna University Press, 1988), 26–31.

[6]*Exegetische Versuche und Besinnungen,* (Göttingen: Vandenhoeck & Ruprecht, 1960), 2:100.

[7]For Jürgen Moltmann, see *Theology of Hope,* trans. James W. Leitch (New York: Harper and Row, 1967); for J. B. Metz, see *Theology of the World,* trans. William Glenn-Doepel (New York: Herder and Herder, 1967).

[8]For a study of Rahner's eschatology, see Phan, *Eternity in Time* (Selinsgrove: Susquehanna University Press, 1988); for a study of von Balthasar's, see John R. Sachs, "Current Eschatology: Universal Salvation and the Problem of Hell," *Theological Studies* 52 (1991): 227–54.

[9]See Peter C. Phan, *Culture and Eschatology: The Iconographical Vision of Paul Evdokimov* (New York: Peter Lang, 1987).

[10]The classic of liberation theology is Gustavo Gutiérrez, *A Theology of Liberation,* trans. Caridad Inda and John Eagleson (Maryknoll, N.Y.: Orbis, 1988). For a discussion of Asian liberation theology, see Peter C. Phan, "Experience and Theology: An Asian Liberation Perspective," *Zeitschrift für Missionswissenschaft und Religionswissenschaft* 77 (1993): 97–121.

[11]For English translations of these two documents, see the bibliography. For a critical evaluation of the second document, see Peter C. Phan, "Contemporary Context and Issues in Eschatology," *Theological Studies* 55 (1994): 507–36.

[12]See Peter C. Phan, "Eschatology and Ecology: The Environment in the End-Time," *Dialogue and Alliance* 9, no. 2 (1995): 99–115.

THE 101 QUESTIONS AND RESPONSES

CHAPTER I
ETERNAL LIFE: HOW DO I KNOW?

Q. 1. Judging from news coverage in secular media such as the press and television, there seems to have been in the United States in the last few decades a heightened interest in what can be called life after death or eternal life. Could you explain this cultural phenomenon?

Despite or, ironically, precisely because of the American obsession with youth, toned-up muscles, and aerobicized bodies, there lurks also in American culture a constant fascination with old age, disease, and death. For every new and improved "youth in a jar" face cream, there is another irremovable wrinkle drawn by the fingers of the Grim Reaper. While this fear and denial of death inadvertently makes the afterlife a permanent fixture of the American scene, in the last two decades, as you have correctly remarked, several factors have contributed to the return of eternal life or life after death as a fashionable topic of conversation among contemporary Americans.

It is not possible to make a complete list of these factors, but at least six deserve special mention. First, there was in the seventies a marked interest in the process of dying sparked by such books as Elisabeth Kübler-Ross' *On Death and Dying* (1970), which described the five stages of dying (denial, anger, bargaining, depression, and acceptance), and Raymond Moody's *Life After Life* (1975), which detailed the experiences of those who were clinically dead but returned to life (near-death experiences). Second, there came an enthrallment with the afterlife and reincarnation, precipitated by the New Age movement with its celebrity advocates, such as Shirley MacLaine with her *Out on a Limb* (1983). Third, there was the "death by choice" or "death with dignity" (euthanasia) movement, with "death doctor" Jack Kevorkian supplying his expertise to those who want to plan and execute their "final exit." Fourth, recent epidemics such as AIDS brought death closer to the attention of the public. Fifth, on a much larger scale, the threat of nuclear destruction and the ecological crisis raised the possibility of the end of human history and of the universe itself. Finally, the sense of an impending cataclysm is further fomented by the approaching end of the millennium, which entices the imagination to revisit past predictions about the end of the world. In sum, these factors, as well as many others, have brought the issue of the afterlife and the ultimate meaning of history once again to the fore.

Q. 2. Given the urgency of these issues, has Christian faith anything to say about them?

As a rule, religions claim to offer answers to questions regarding the beyond and to help their followers attain ultimate happiness, variously referred to as heaven, paradise, eternal life, or nirvana. Christianity is no exception. One of the central tenets of its creed proclaims that its founder, Jesus Christ, who died and was raised to life, will come again to judge the living and the dead and that there will be the resurrection of the dead and life everlasting.

Christian systematic and critical reflection on these truths is called *eschatology*, literally, speech or discourse *(logos)* on the last thing *(eschaton)* or last things *(eschata)*. So central is the belief in eternal life to the Christian faith (and by implication, eschatology to theology) that Karl Barth (1886–1968), an influential Protestant theologian, has defined their mutual relationship in a memorable dictum: "Christianity that is not entirely and altogether eschatology has entirely and altogether nothing to do with Christ" (*The Epistle to the Romans,* 314).

Q. 3. If eschatology is so central to Christian faith, how come one rarely hears Catholic preachers talk about it these days?

In the pre-Vatican II theology often referred to as neo-scholastic, eschatology as a theological tract taught in the seminary had a rather standard structure. Called *De Novissimis,* that is, *On the Last Things,* it dealt almost exclusively with the eternal fate of the individual. In particular, it discussed how the individual person meets the four Last Things, namely, death, judgment, heaven, and hell. Appropriately enough, the topic was regularly placed at the end of the theological curriculum, almost like an appendix. As a result, its relationship to the other articles of Christian faith and daily life was often left undeveloped.

Furthermore, not rarely did it indulge in fanciful speculations on the afterlife, with little relevance for Christian living. Theologians expended their energies arguing about the nature of purgatorial fire, the possible maximum length of the stay in purgatory, the nature of limbo, the kinds of pains in hell, the characteristics of the risen body, the location of heaven and hell, and so on. Christian eschatology acquired a distinctly individualistic and otherworldly cast. Yves Congar (1904–95), a French Dominican theologian and cardinal, called this approach to eschatology "the physical style," that is, it regards the last realities as things rather than as processes affecting the person and society.

Of course, this approach did not prevent preachers from using the eschatological doctrines, especially in their fire-and-brimstone sermons during parish missions, to frighten wayward Christians back to the straight and narrow path toward heaven. This misuse and abuse of eschatology, combined with the overly individualistic and otherworldly casting of this doctrine, were among the factors that eventually brought about the silence of many preachers about the afterlife that your question alluded to.

There are also other reasons why contemporary preachers and religious teachers are reluctant to speak of the afterlife, at least in the customary ways. One is that we are aware that biblical and traditional affirmations about the afterlife cannot be taken literally, in the way many fundamentalists are wont to do, and that makes our speaking about heaven and hell much more difficult. Furthermore, the realization that the good news that Jesus came to proclaim is about the salvation of sinners, not their damnation, has led many preachers to avoid speaking about hell.

Q. 4. Does this mean that this eclipse of eschatology in contemporary Christian discourse is something inevitable and perhaps to be welcomed?

Not at all. It means, however, that in order to make our doctrine about the afterlife understandable and credible to our contemporaries, we have to overcome the individualism and otherworldliness that characterize its traditional formulation. There is a consensus among historians of Christian doctrine that during the first millennium reflections on the afterlife focused primarily on the collective dimension of salvation. While holding fast to the grace of salvation already brought about by Jesus' life, death, and resurrection, Christian faith and hope resolutely directed the believers' gaze to Christ's imminent return *(parousia)*, at which time the dead will rise, the final judgment will be pronounced, the whole created order will be transformed, and Christ will hand his kingdom over to his Father, so that God may be "all in all" (1 Cor 15:28).

In the in-between time, from Christ's ascension to his glorious return, the church is a pilgrim people living in hope, responding to God's gift of self, in the power and under the guidance of the Holy Spirit, so that the kingdom of God may be realized in the world. In other words, eschatology was centered on Christ (christological), the church (ecclesial), and the cosmos (cosmic). These are the dimensions that must be retrieved in our reconstruction of eschatology.

Furthermore, we need to explain more clearly the intimate connections between eschatology and the other parts of theology, such as the doctrine of God, the theology of the sacraments, and Christian life in general. For example, we need to ask what the role of the Holy Spirit is in the final fulfillment of all things in the kingdom of God; we must make clear how the Eucharist is the sacrament of hope par excellence in which, as Vatican II's Constitution on the Liturgy says, "a pledge of future glory is given to us" (*Sacrosanctum Concilium,* no. 47), and in which we proclaim Christ's death and resurrection "until he comes again"; and we must show the ways in which our graced Christian existence is an anticipation and a foretaste of eternal life. In this way, eschatology will appear not as an irrelevant appendix to theology but as its center, conferring full meaning to other Christian truths.

We must also emphasize, besides the personal and interpersonal aspects of human existence, its sociopolitical and economic dimensions. Human beings are social animals by nature. Questions must then be raised about the relationship, for instance, between Christian hope and this-worldly utopias, between salvation from sin and liberation from economic and political oppression, between liturgical worship and social activities, between church and world, between history and the kingdom of God, and between this universe that is our home and the perfected cosmos. If an intrinsic connection can be shown to exist between these sets of polarities, belief in the afterlife will not be seen as an opium of the people to soothe their existential anxieties or as an escape from their historical responsibilities; rather, as Vatican II says in its Pastoral Constitution on the Church in the Modern World, "far from diminishing our concern to develop this earth, the expectancy of a new earth should spur us on, for it is here that the body of a new human family grows, foreshadowing in some way the age which is to come" (*Gaudium et Spes,* no. 39).

Q. 5. Even if eschatology can be rendered more credible by retrieving the various dimensions you have just explained, there still remains the problem of how to understand the statements made by the Bible and Tradition about the afterlife, since you have said above that they cannot be taken literally. How, indeed, should one take them? For instance, how should one understand the texts that say that there will be "grinding of teeth" as a form of punishment for sin (see Mt 8:12; 22:13; 25:30)?

The example you cited reminds me of an apocryphal story about a preacher who in his zeal to convert sinners threatened the unrepentant ones with the eternal pains of "grinding of teeth." He was, however, frustrated by one of the men in the audience who kept smiling smugly rather than shaking with fear as expected. After the sermon, when the preacher asked him why he was not overtaken by fear of divine retribution, the man gleefully replied that he had lost all his teeth and was wearing dentures. The crafty preacher retorted, "Teeth will be immediately provided!"

All joking aside, however, your question poses one of the thorniest problems in theology in general and eschatology in particular. It concerns the interpretation of the Bible and Tradition, which is referred to as hermeneutics. Because your question deals with a very complex issue, I will answer it in stages. First of all, we need to discuss briefly what is involved in interpretation in general, then in biblical interpretation, and finally in the interpretation of eschatological statements. In this answer I will deal with what is going on when we perform the act of interpretation.

Scholars such as German philosopher Hans-Georg Gadamer and French thinker Paul Ricoeur have pointed out that when we attempt to understand a text, a work of art, an event, or anything at all, we enter the subject matter to be understood with some *preunderstanding* or *prejudgment* of it. This preunderstanding is formed by the tradition of (often conflicting) interpretations of this subject matter and gives a handle on it. This tradition, combined with the sense that everything (both the interpreter and the reality to be interpreted) exists within the flux of time and history (the historical consciousness), is what Gadamer calls the "effective historical consciousness." Of course, the reality to be interpreted has already caught our attention and interest because of the promise of meaning and truth we dimly perceive in it. In this sense it can be called a "classic," as David Tracy, an American theologian suggests.

In the act of interpretation, therefore, there is an interaction among three realities: the phenomenon to be understood (primarily texts in literate societies), the interpreter, and the process of interpreting itself.

The first element, the reality to be interpreted, which is sometimes elevated to the status of classic, (1) takes on a particular form from its surrounding culture (e.g., baroque art); (2) bears both permanence and excess of meaning (e.g., the vision of beauty captured and conveyed by the artist but somehow eluding him or her), and therefore gives rise to a plurality of interpretations and resists definitive interpretation; (3) is particular in its history of production (e.g., in Italy, in the eighteenth century) but can be universal in its effect and therefore is susceptible to appreciation everywhere today; and (4) is subject to varying reception and so can be canonized at one time (e.g., prescribed readings in a college course) and forgotten or repressed at another (e.g., when baroque art is out of favor).

In the case of a *written* text, as opposed to an oral speech, the text (1) begins to have a life of its own, independent from the author's intention, and takes on meanings not intended by its author, thus gaining a "semantic autonomy"; (2) goes beyond the original audience and addresses anyone who reads it, thereby acquiring a universal audience; and (3) moves beyond the original situation, allowing itself to be removed from its original context and inserted into ever new situations. The text is therefore potentially universal.

The second element, that is, the interpreter, comes to the text to be interpreted with a preunderstanding that is part of his or her tradition. The text is recognized in its strangeness and otherness and with its claim to meaning and truth. The interpreter is willing to critically distance himself or herself from his or her familiar traditions and to let the otherness and the strange meaning and truth of the text suspect, challenge, correct, and enrich his or her preunderstanding embodied in the tradition. By the same token, the perceived meaning of the text and the presuppositions under which the text was produced may be suspected, challenged, corrected, and enriched in their turn.

The interpreter is neither totally passive, docilely absorbing the possible meaning and truth of the classic, nor totally active, freely creating meaning and truth at will. Nor will the meaning of the classic remain the same. The classic and the interpreter interact in a give-and-take, back-and-forth process of interpreting. The interpreter interprets the classic, and the classic interprets the interpreter; neither remains unchanged in the process. The new meaning emerges or is disclosed when the interpreter critically correlates his or her present world of experience with the world projected by the text.

The third element of the interpretive act is the process of interpretation itself. It has been compared to a game or a conversation. To be successful, the game must have its own rules to which the players must conform and must possess its own movement to which the players abandon themselves. The conversation is itself a kind of game in which the subject matter or the question itself, and not the opinions and interests of the conversation partners, determines the rhythm and outcome of the conversation. Analogously, the interpreter must follow certain rules so as to discern the meaning and truth that the classic discloses in its encounter with the interpreter.

Q. 6. I now understand that interpretation is a complex process of interaction among the reality to be interpreted, the interpreter, and the act of interpreting itself. But how does that process apply to the interpretation of the Bible?

I hope I have shown that any act of interpretation is a complex process of dialogue between the reader and the text, which is personally engaged, socially situated, and historically conditioned. It is particularly important that we remember this when we undertake the task of interpreting the Bible and its eschatological statements because there is a constant temptation (and a frequent practice) of ignoring what has been said above about interpretation and assuming that what is needed is just to take a look at what the Bible says. Somehow, it is believed, the meaning of the Bible leaps off its pages.

If the meaning of even a contemporary text cannot be grasped just by taking a look, much less so can that of the books of the Bible. Do not forget that the Bible is a library of books written thousands of years ago, in languages hardly known to most of us and by people who lived in foreign places and cultures. Hence, we need rules or methods to bridge the geographical, temporal, linguistic, and cultural distance that separates us from those who wrote the Bible and those to whom they wrote. After all, the writers of the Bible did not envision our circumstances, nor did they write *to* us, even though what they wrote continues to make sense to us as well.

With regard to the rules or methods of interpreting the Bible, Vatican II in its Constitution on Divine Revelation has laid down some very useful guidelines. The text of *Dei Verbum,* number 12, is rather long, so I will summarize its main ideas. First, we must attempt to find out what the biblical writers wanted to convey and did convey through the medium of their words (the literal or literary meaning). Second, in order to do so, we must pay attention to their customary and characteristic patterns of perception, speech, and narrative (the literary forms) and to the conventions that their contemporaries followed in their dealings with one another. Third, because the Bible is not only human words but also God's word, we must read the Bible as a whole. This means that we must read what we call the Old Testament in light of the New and vice versa, and one biblical book in light of another, because God is the "author" of the entire Bible. Finally, we must take into account the interpretations that have been given by Tradition, in particular by those who have been commissioned to give an authoritative interpretation of the Bible (the magisterium). We must also take care that our interpretations do not contradict the certain beliefs of the church (the analogy of faith).

Q. 7. In practice, what are the steps I must follow to interpret the Bible?

The Bible is the sacred written record of the words God spoke to us and of the deeds God performed for us in history. Because it is a historical, literary, and revelatory text, its interpretation involves three interrelated steps.

First, because it is a historical document, we must apply *historical criticism* in order to ascertain what the text said, that is, the meaning of the text. This meaning is often called the "literal (literary) meaning" (not literalist meaning, but the meaning intended by the author and conveyed by his or her words) or the "plain sense." The goal of this phase is to *explain* the text by determining its "ideal meaning." This meaning is made up of both sense (what the word says in a proposition, e.g., reign of God) and reference (what the proposition claims to be true, e.g., the reign of God has already come). In performing this work of exegesis, several methods and techniques are used, among them *textual* criticism (to determine the authenticity and transmission of the text); *source* criticism (to discern the possible influence of one text upon another); *form* criticism (to investigate the origin and history of the oral traditions behind the Bible, the communities in which it took shape, and the various literary genres in which it is written); and *redaction* criticism (to identify the stages of the composition of the Bible by its authors and the creative role of the writers in editing, combining, and shaping the traditions they inherited). In this phase the Bible is used as a *window* through which the reader looks at the world *behind* the text.

Secondly, because the Bible is also a linguistic and literary work, *literary* criticism must also be applied to understand the text as a literary artifact, what it intends to do with the readers, and how well it accomplishes its goals. More specifically, since the Bible is a book of witness, it is analyzed to determine how well it carries out its task of witnessing to the readers through its structure, its literary forms, and its contents.

A variety of methods and techniques have been used for this purpose. Some scholars have examined the Bible as a book of stories (narrative criticism); others, its art of persuasion (rhetorical criticism); others, its use of parables (parable research); others, its use of the letter genre (epistolary analysis); and others still, its impact upon the readers (reader-response criticism).

In this phase, the Bible is seen as a *mirror* in which the reader discovers herself or himself. The focus is placed on the world *of* the text. In a true sense of the word, the text is an *art object,* and remains so unless and until it is interpreted; then it becomes a *work of art.* Just as a visual art object (e.g., Michelangelo's "Pietà") only becomes a work of art when it is contemplated; just as a musical score (e.g., Beethoven's "Moonlight Sonata") does not become music until it is played; and just as a script (e.g., Shakespeare's *Hamlet*) does not become a drama until it is performed, so the Bible does not become the word of God for the reader until she or he interprets it. Then the Bible reveals a possible alternative world or reality and opens up for the reader a new way of being, a different possibility of existence that he or she must accept or reject.

Thirdly, since the Bible is a sacred book, written not only to inform but also and primarily to *transform* the reader, the process of interpretation must move beyond explaining and understanding the Bible to *appropriating* the meaning of the Bible. In this way the reader comes to own its ideal meaning, which then becomes the existential meaning for the reader. The worlds *behind* and *of* the Bible have projected a world *in front of* the Bible, that is, a new way of being and acting, into which the reader is invited to enter and make his or her own. We can call this third step of interpretation "hermeneutics" to distinguish it from exegesis (the first step) and criticism (the second step).

Thus, the reader/interpreter must perform a twofold task. First, just as the critic of the visual arts or music or drama has to stand away from the work of art to evaluate its colors or sound or action, so the reader approaches the text in a critical manner, distancing from it so as to determine its ideal meaning by means of historical and literary criticism, and even to unmask its distorting ideologies.

Second, just as the critic cannot fully enjoy the beauty of a painting or a symphony or a play unless she or he aesthetically surrenders herself or himself to the work of art, so the reader, to fully understand the text, must enter the world projected by the text, that is, the world *in front of* the text, and appropriate its meaning existentially. What will hopefully occur then is a multidimentional conversion, a transformative interpretation, a new spirituality on the part of the reader, who will acquire not only a new understanding of the Bible but also a new way of seeing the world and of being and acting in the world. Only then will the act of interpretation be completed.

Q. 8. I now understand that biblical interpretation is a complex process of discovering the worlds behind, in, and in front of the text. But how does one interpret biblical statements about the afterlife in particular?

Christian theology, and by implication Christian eschatology, must be rooted in Scripture and Tradition. Hence, Christian eschatology must carefully examine and interpret what the Bible and Tradition have to say about the ultimate destiny of the individual (personal eschatology), the Israelite people (national eschatology), the human family (collective eschatology), and the world (cosmic eschatology).

With regard to biblical eschatology in particular, we must bring to bear upon it the various methods mentioned above. First, using *historical* criticism, we must, by means of textual criticism, determine the authenticity of biblical eschatological statements. Then, by means of source criticism, their historicity will have to be determined and their influence, if any, on one another will have to be discerned. Next, by means of form criticism, we have to inquire about the kinds of communities in which these statements were formed orally before they were written down, and, most importantly, we have to examine the literary genres in which they are expressed and identify the characteristics of these genres. Finally, by means of redaction criticism, we will have to study how a particular author selects, synthesizes, and incorporates these various sayings into his own work in view of the audience he addresses. In this way we hope to arrive at the ideal meaning of these statements and reach the world *behind* them.

Secondly, taking these eschatological statements in their *literary* context, we will have to ask what they intend to do and how well they do their self-appointed task. For example, it will be asked whether they intend to give readers a preview of the afterlife or whether they function to give us a *warning* about how we should live in order to receive eternal life. In other words, we will try to enter into the world *of* these eschatological assertions to discover what they can tell us, their new audience, now, in our contemporary context, with our own concerns and questions.

Third, because we believe that these eschatological statements reveal God and the divine plan of salvation to us, we will ask what kind of life and action they propose to us, that is, the world *in front of* them. We hope to fuse our own horizon of understanding with theirs so that we may understand not only what they *meant* when they were written but also what they *mean* to us today. In this way we will be able to achieve a transformative understanding of these texts; that is, their ideal meaning will become our existential meaning.

Of course, because of space limitations, we will not be able to perform this threefold interpretive task equally for all biblical and traditional affirmations about the afterlife. In the next chapter I will treat of biblical eschatology in general and will postpone treatment of its various specific affirmations (e.g., on death, resurrection, judgment, hell, heaven, and so on) to the chapters that deal with these particular themes.

Q. 9. Before you tell us what the Bible has to say about the afterlife, please explain some of the key concepts people use to speak of the afterlife, such as eternity or eternal life. What do you mean by eternity? How is it related to our time?

To understand what is meant by eternity, it would be helpful to clarify briefly what we mean by time. By time we usually mean, as the Greek philosopher Aristotle has said, the measurement of before and after in motion and change, that is, the succession of moments. This time is measured by clocks and calendars and constitutes chronology (the Greeks use the term *chronos* to designate this kind of time). In this understanding of time, only the present as a durationless instant exists;

the past no longer exists because it is already gone, and the future does not yet exist because it is still to come.

Besides this physical conception of time, there is another meaning of time that is rooted in interior human experience. We human beings who live in the present do not experience the past as something irretrievably lost and gone but as truly present, effectively shaping our identity and our destiny. Similarly, we do not experience the future merely as something empty and unreal; we experience it as a lure and a challenge, inviting us to move forward to actualize our potentialities. In this human time, the past is gathered up and preserved in our *memory,* and the future is anticipated and made real in our *imagination* and *expectation.* In this time, not every moment is of equal worth and importance; rather, there are decisive moments for one's existence (the Greeks use the word *kairos* to designate this kind of time as opposed to time as *chronos*). Thus, when we are in pain, an hour is much longer than sixty minutes, whereas when we are enjoying ourselves, time seems to fly by.

As Augustine has said, in time our soul is "distended," turning backward to embrace the past, and reaching forward to anticipate future possibilities. Our identity is achieved by this capacity to somehow fuse the three layers of time—past, present, and future—into a personal unity and to possess all three dimensions of time wholly and together. Of course, as long as we live in time, such a personal unity and possession of time is only partially realized and necessarily remains a distant goal. Nevertheless, it is a goal we constantly strive for. To live in time, then, is to be engaged in this movement from incompleteness to completeness, to transcend the division and fragmentariness of time toward its wholeness and unity.

This reality of wholeness and unity beyond the division and fragmentariness of time is called *eternity.* In contrast to time as sequential measurement of change, eternity is defined by Boethius, a sixth-century Roman philosopher, as "the instantaneously whole and complete possession of endless life." Such eternity is predicated exclusively of God, because only God has neither beginning nor end, neither before nor after, and is not by necessity subject to change. Eternity is therefore fullness or perfection of life and being, without decay and succession.

In this sense eternity is not a pure negation of time. On the contrary, Christian revelation affirms that in the incarnation of God's Son,

God has freely and out of love assumed human temporality, time, and change and has raised them into divine life. In and through this action, God also allows human beings to share in God's own fullness of life or eternal life. In this way, the human drive to overcome the division and fragmentariness of time and to gather up one's past, present, and future in unity and wholeness, which would be frustrated if left to itself, is given fulfillment by God's gracious condescension to eternalize time.

Eternity then should not be imagined as an endless continuation of time beyond death, as never-ending time running on and on in the other world, as the expression "for ever and ever" may suggest. For then, we cannot understand how eternal life or heaven is bliss, since we are doomed as it were to roam forever, in search of a final destination, without ever "coming home." Rather, our sharing in God's eternity means that our own time and history are made final, irrevocable, and definitive by God. In this sense our participated eternity is not outside, above, after, or beyond our time; rather, it is achieved *in* and *from* our time.

Q. 10. Granted that our eternity is a share in God's eternity, how can our time be made eternity?

One way to understand the process in which our time is transformed into eternity is to consider how we exercise our freedom. Thanks to our freedom, human beings can make choices for this or that course of action, for this or that thing. In principle, these choices can be reversed. I may decide to go the movies and then decide to read a novel instead. I may decide to hate my enemies and then relent and forgive them. In and through these myriad decisions, as the German theologian Karl Rahner (1904–84) has pointed out, we do not simply do this or that but ultimately we *become who we are*.

Freedom as freedom to *become oneself* and not just *to do something* is by its very nature the person's ability to determine himself or herself once and for all, definitively, and finally. Through our freely willed actions, we become who we want to be forever. These actions shape our character and identity and determine our eternal destiny. Of course, as long as we are alive, our character and destiny remain not yet definitively determined; they can be molded in one direction at one time and in a different direction at another. But in and through our particular choices, they are being continuously shaped, and the final shape will be made definitive and irreversible, as we will see later, in our dying and death. This final, definitive, and irreversible shape of our identity and destiny, when received and ratified by God, is our "eternity."

There is an intrinsic unity among the triad of time, freedom, and eternity. Time makes freedom possible, freedom confers meaning to time, and eternity is time made final and definitive by freedom.

Q. 11. I anticipate that in the following pages you will speak of many things concerning the afterlife. But to avoid missing the forest for the trees, could you tell me what eschatology is all about?

It is true that we will discuss a lot of things about the afterlife, and indeed we must speak not only about what will happen to the human family and the cosmos in general (collective eschatology) but also about what will occur to the individual (individual eschatology). But, as you correctly point out, because we will have to speak about so many and diverse things, there is the danger of losing sight of the center of all theology and, consequently, of eschatology. That center is the Triune God.

As the Swiss theologian Hans Urs von Balthasar (1905–88), paraphrasing Augustine, has put it tersely and elegantly: "God is 'the last thing' for the creature. Gained, God is heaven; lost, hell; testing, judgment; purifying, purgatory. God himself is that in which the finite dies and through which it rises again in God and to God. God himself is such that God turns himself to the world, namely, in his Son Jesus Christ, who is the manifestation of God and therefore also the sum of the 'last things'" (*Fragen der Theologie Heute*, 407–8).

What we have to remember then is that God and only God, whose blessed life has been given to us, is the center of eschatology. To every statement about the destiny of the individual person, the society, and the cosmos, we must pose this question: What does it say implicitly about the character of God? If what it affirms of God is consistent with the truths we know about God, then it is true. This is a helpful criterion to determine the truth of every eschatological assertion we may come across.

Q. 12. Besides God, von Balthasar's statement also mentions Jesus Christ as "the sum of the 'last things.'" What is the role of Jesus in eschatology?

Whereas God is the ultimate subject matter of eschatology, insofar as it is really about God that eschatological statements speak, Jesus' life, teaching, and especially resurrection are both the cause of our eternal life and the source of whatever we know about the afterlife. As Paul says, "If there is no resurrection of the dead, then neither has Christ been raised. And if Christ has not been raised, then empty [too] is our preaching; empty, too, your faith" (1 Cor 15:13–14). If we want to express all this in philosophical terms, we may say that God is the material principle and Jesus is the formal principle of eschatology.

As the formal principle of eschatology, Christ is both the *cause* and the *model* of our own resurrection and our eternal life. Christ is the cause of our resurrection and eternal life insofar as, thanks to him and because of him, what God has done for his Son in his resurrection and glorification God will also do for us, God's adopted children and Jesus' sisters and brothers. Christ is also the model of our eternal life because in order to know what will happen to us in the afterlife, we must look to what has happened to the risen Jesus.

In this sense, eschatology may be said to be nothing more than an interpretation of the future human and cosmic fulfillment in the light of Christ. As Karl Rahner puts it, "Christ himself is the hermeneutical principle of all eschatological assertions. Anything that cannot be read and understood as a christological assertion is not a genuine eschatological assertion" (*Theological Investigations,* 4:342–43).

Q. 13. Besides Christology, is there any other theological discipline that serves as a norm and source for eschatology?

Yes, and that is liturgy and worship. There is a saying attributed to Prosper of Aquitaine (ca. 390–ca. 463) that affirms that "the law of prayer establishes the law of belief" *(legem credendi lex statuit supplicandi,* often abbreviated as *lex orandi, lex credendi).* The meaning of this principle is that when the church prays and celebrates the sacraments, it confesses the faith received from the apostles. That is, the church believes as it prays. Consequently, in elaborating theology in general and eschatology in particular, attention must be paid to the liturgical "text" to determine what the church believes, explicitly and implicitly. The liturgical text includes not only the liturgical books but also the liturgical rites, past and present, as well as the actual celebrations of these rites. For example, to understand what the church believes about death and dying, we have to examine the liturgical books such as those about the sacrament of anointing of the sick and funerals, the rituals of anointing and burial, and the actual ways in which particular communities celebrate these rites.

The reverse should also be undertaken, that is, one must critically examine the rites and their actual celebrations to ascertain whether they faithfully enact the belief of the church. In this sense, it must be said that the law of belief establishes the law of prayer *(lex credendi, lex orandi)*. For example, we must ask whether certain prayers for the souls in purgatory reflect correctly the belief of the church about purgatory or whether certain liturgical formulations regarding hell express accurately the church's belief in the universal saving will of God (see 1 Tm 2:4).

CHAPTER II
BIBLICAL ESCHATOLOGY:
THE END-TIME ACCORDING
TO THE SCRIPTURES

Q. 14. In what sense can you say that there is an eschatological doctrine in the Hebrew Scriptures or the Old Testament?

If by eschatology is meant the doctrine of the four Last Things—death, judgment, heaven, and hell—then the Hebrew Scriptures, which Christians call the Old Testament, do not as a whole offer a fully developed eschatology. Of course, the Old Testament (which is seven books larger than the Hebrew Scriptures) does speak about death, but it is rather reticent about the afterlife. No hope of individual survival after death is expressed in the Old Testament except in some late texts written probably in the second century B.C.E. I will discuss the various teachings of the Old Testament on the afterlife in future questions. Suffice it to point out here that whatever eschatological doctrine the Hebrew Scriptures have, it is rooted in the Israelites' hope for a future salvation proclaimed first by the prophets and then by the apocalytic writers.

Q. 15. How is the hope in future salvation proclaimed by the prophets related to eschatology?

Though popularly associated with ecstatic trances and predictions of the future, the classical Hebrew prophets (e.g., Amos, Hosea, Isaiah, and Micah) were primarily concerned with discerning and interpreting God's will for their contemporaries, especially in view of their transgressions against God's commandments given in the covenant. They announced "the day of Yahweh" on which God would punish the people for their unfaithfulness. Divine punishment was regularly described in terms of natural disasters, loss of monarchy and priesthood, exile from the land, desecration of the Temple, profanation of the cult, and oppression of all kinds.

Paradoxically, however, God's judgment and punishment are the source of *hope.* Divine chastisements were not intended to destroy the people but were presented as necessary medicine to heal them. They served to remind the people of God's loving kindness *(hesed)* toward them and to make them mend their ways in order to find God's favor again. In the end God's love and fidelity *(emet)* will carry the day in spite of human failures.

This unshakable hope in God's future and definitive victory over evil was rekindled by the postexilic prophets, for example, Jeremiah; Ezekiel; Second Isaiah (40–55); Third Isaiah (56–65); Isaiah (24–27 [the so-called Isaiah apocalypse]); Haggai; and Zechariah. Though they still vigorously denounced the people for their idolatry and unfaithfulness to Yahweh, these prophets announced the imminent coming of a new age in which God would intervene to save God's people.

This promised salvation would be brought about either directly by God or by means of an intermediary, variously named the Suffering Servant or the Messiah, who would be a priest or king or prophet. This new age was described as a replication of some past significant events. It was characterized as a new creation, a new exodus, a new covenant, the reunification of the nation, the restoration of the Davidic dynasty, the rebuilding of Jerusalem and the Temple, the restoration of the true cult, and a complete observation of the Torah. This new age was called "the kingdom of God," in which God rules not only over Israel but also over the nations and the cosmos in truth, justice, and peace.

Through their preaching and writings the Hebrew prophets created what may be termed *prophetic eschatology.* Even though, from the literary standpoint, it is inappropriate to refer to the prophetic writings as *eschatological literature,* nevertheless they can be seen as a common body of writings marked by the following features. First, there is a pessimistic assessment of the present order as pervaded by sin and evil, followed by a prediction of divine punishment. Second, there are fantastic and extravagant descriptions of the new age with stock-in-trade themes and imagery, as mentioned above. Third, there is a stark contrast between the present age and the age to come. Increasingly, the new age was seen less as a recovery of the ideal past than as a destruction of the present order, an annihilation of God's enemies, and a creation of a totally new world beyond history and this cosmos. Fourth, attempts were made to specify the time when the prophecy would be fulfilled. Jeremiah and Ezekiel were the first to do so, and Second Isaiah linked the coming of the new age with a historical event, namely, King Cyrus' permission granted to the Jews to go back to their homeland. Third Isaiah, Haggai, and Zechariah saw God's intervention as imminent.

In sum, prophetic eschatology was not concerned with the fate of the individual but with the destination of the Israelite nation as a whole. It was nourished by the indestructible hope in the eschatological salvation based upon God's promise to Abraham and his progeny (the patriarchal promise traditions), to the people of Israel in the covenant (the Sinai Covenant traditions), and to David and his dynasty (the David-Zion traditions).

But the ideal and at times idyllic description of the eschatological age far outstrips reality. Bitter disappointments poisoned the wellspring of hope when, as we read in the fifth-century writings of Malachi, Ezra, and Nehemiah, the restored Temple, cult, and priesthood were seen as polluted, and the people continued to violate the Torah. Hope was not given up, however, even with the loss of national independence under the domination of the Greeks, first the Ptolemies, and then the Seleucids (332–160 B.C.E.). On the contrary, a new form of literature was about to emerge to give a different voice to this hope. These writings are called *apocalyptic* literature, which has its distinct eschatology.

Q. 16. Besides the prophets, you have also mentioned apocalyptic writers in the Old Testament as contributing to its eschatology. What is apocalypticism, and which are the apocalyptic books in the Bible?

It is helpful to distinguish between *apocalypse* as a literary genre, *apocalyptic eschatology* as a religious worldview, and *apocalypticism* as a social ideology using apocalyptic eschatology as the organizational principle of a community or movement (e.g., the Qumran community).

As a literary genre, apocalypse (from the Greek *apocalypsis,* meaning revelation, disclosure) is well defined by the opening three verses of the only apocalyptic book of the New Testament: "The revelation of Jesus Christ, which God gave to him, to show his servants what must happen soon. He made it known by sending his angel to his servant John, who gives witness to the word of God and to the testimony of Jesus Christ by reporting what he saw. Blessed is the one who reads aloud and blessed are those who listen to this prophetic message and heed what is written in it, for the appointed time is near" (Rv 1:1–2).

Here we have the essential elements of the apocalyptic genre: (1) it is a *revelation* given by God or Jesus Christ; (2) through an other-worldly *mediator,* for example, an angel; (3) to a human *seer* or *prophet,* for example, John; (4) disclosing *future, imminent events,* for example, the final judgment by God; and (5) containing an *admonition,* for example, exhortation to steadfastness during persecutions.

John J. Collins, who has studied all the apocalyptical texts from 250 B.C.E. to 250 C.E., defines *apocalypsis* as follows: "'Apocalypse' is a genre of revelatory literature with a narrative framework, in which a revelation is mediated by an otherworldly being to a human recipient, disclosing a transcendent reality which is both temporal, insofar as it envisages eschatological salvation, and spatial, insofar as it involves another, supernatural world" (*The Apocalyptic Imagination,* 4).

In the Bible there are two books that belong to this genre, Daniel in the Old Testament and Revelation in the New Testament. Some extracanonical writings also belong to it, notably *First Enoch, Second Enoch, Syriac Apocalypse of Baruch, Greek Apocalypse of Baruch, Apocalypse of Ezra, Apocalypse of Abraham,* and *Ascension of Isaiah.*

Q. 17. Which are the characteristics of these apocalyptic writings?

To answer this question correctly, it is important, as we have said in the last chapter, to attend to the kind of historical setting in which these writings were composed, the function they were intended to perform, and the language they used to express their contents. Though it is not true that all the apocalyptic literature was produced by a single movement, much less by a sectarian conventicle, in general most apocalypses were written in a situation of crisis and alienation of diverse kinds. These situations include loss of national independence, social powerlessness, and persecution, both religious and political, by a foreign power, for example, the rule of the Seleucids, especially Antiochus IV Epiphanes.

One principal function of apocalyptic literature was to exhort those who were alienated from the power structures of this world and oppressed for their religious belief and to assure them that God will ultimately vindicate and save them. It does so by directing the eyes of the suffering people away from the distressful present and focus their attention on the heavenly world and the eschatological future. Another function may be simply to promote a particular worldview and to encourage people to think and act in line with that worldview.

As might be expected, the language of apocalyptic literature is highly imaginative, even fantastic. Mostly pseudonymous, these writings make extensive use of visions, heavenly journeys, secret books, and angelic revelations to convey their message. John J. Collins has singled out two characteristics of this language. First, it is not descriptive but *expressive:* "The language of the apocalypses is not descriptive, referential newspaper language, but the *expressive* language of poetry, which uses symbols and imagery to articulate a sense or feeling about the world. Their abiding value does not lie in the pseudoinformation they provide about cosmology or future history, but in the affirmation of a transcendent world" (*The Apocalyptic Imagination,* 214). Consequently, it would be wrong to use the apocalypses to paint a scenario of the end of the world or to describe what will happen in the other world.

Second, apocalyptic language is not only expressive but also *commissive,* that is, pragmatic and oriented toward action. It commits the readers to a view of the world that demands a change in attitude and corresponding actions: "It is far more congenial to the pragmatic tendency of liberation theology, which is not engaged in the pursuit of objective truth but in the dynamics of motivation and the exercise of political power" (*The Apocalyptic Imagination,* 215). To use the language of hermeneutics discussed in Question 7, apocalyptic literature requires not only historical exegesis and literary criticism but also existential hermeneutics.

Q. 18. What, then, does the apocalypse say about eschatology, and how is it related to the prophetic movement?

The perspective of apocalyptic eschatology can best be understood as an outgrowth, though not necessarily chronological, from prophetic eschatology. Both eschatologies are the two sides of the same coin. Concerned with the people's unfaithfulness to the covenant, prophetic eschatology tends to emphasize the need for human efforts at conversion to God, whereas apocalyptic eschatology, born in times of extreme distress and suffering, tends to be pessimistic about the effectiveness of human reform and social institutions in general. Hence, apocalyptic eschatology includes a powerful rhetoric for denouncing the deficiencies of this world and proposes a revolutionary imaginative construal of an alternative world. Its vision is radically dualistic; it entails the destruction of this present world and the resurrection of the faithful to a blessed existence in the future, transcendent world.

Thus, the characteristic contents of apocalyptic eschatology are (1) a fervent belief in the supernatural world with its detailed descriptions of heavenly regions, angelic beings, the abodes of the dead, the places of judgment, and fallen angels; and (2) an eager anticipation of the final salvation with its distinctively new beliefs in the judgment of the dead and the resurrection of the faithful into glory.

For instance, Daniel, a representative sample of the "historical" apocalypses written during the persecution by Antiochus IV Epiphanes (175–164 B.C.E.), presents a vision in which the beasts (i.e., foreign powers, especially Antiochus IV Epiphanes) were slain, and "one like a son of man" (i.e., the people of Israel or an angelic being), coming on the clouds of heaven, proceeded to the throne of the "Ancient One" to receive "dominion, glory and kingship" (Dn 7). Furthermore, Daniel envisions that when Michael, "the great prince, guardian of your people," arises, all the people whose names are inscribed in the book will be delivered. Then, "many of those who sleep/in the dust of the earth shall awake;/Some shall live forever,/others shall be an everlasting horror and disgrace./But the wise shall shine brightly/like the splendor of the firmament,/And those who lead the many to justice/shall be like the stars forever" (Dn 12:1–3). Incidentally, this is the first text in the Old Testament (and the only one in the Hebrew Bible) that explicitly affirms the resurrection of the dead. Fundamental to Daniel and apocalyptic eschatology are the beliefs that events are guided by higher powers, that the course of history is predetermined and its end assured, and that the destiny of the wise lies beyond this life and pertains to the world of angels.

Q. 19. Did such prophetic and apocalyptic eschatology have any effect on the Jewish people at the time?

It is only to be expected that these currents of thought should have an influence on the Jewish community. At least one segment of this society, that is, the Qumran community, was deeply influenced by the apocalyptic worldview of Daniel and Enoch. The Qumran community, located near the Dead Sea and discovered in 1947, was most probably constituted by the Essenes and lasted from the second century B.C.E. to 68 C.E. These pious Jews, who had maintained fidelity to the covenant during the persecution by Antiochus IV Epiphanes, rejected the Hasmonean dynasty for its compromises with the Seleucids, especially regarding the priesthood, and withdrew to the desert of Judea under the leadership of one whom they called the "Teacher of Righteousness." There, in a highly ascetical life, they prepared for the end-time, which, according to them, would be marked by the rise of the three figures foretold by the Old Testament, that is, the prophet like Moses, the Davidic Messiah, and the priest of Aaron's line.

According to the Qumran exegetes, the prophets knew by divine revelation what God would do at the end-time, but they did not know *when* the end-time would come. On the contrary, their Teacher of Righteousness had received from God's revelation this additional piece of information and communicated it to his followers. It would seem that for them, the end-time would come very soon, perhaps within their generation.

Q. 20. Was Jesus also influenced by Jewish apocalypticism?

In recent scholarship on the historical Jesus, special attention has been paid to the Jewish eschatology as the context for his life and teaching. Jesus began his life in a time of great political unrest that was ripe for intense apocalyptic expectations: following the death of Herod the Great in 4 B.C.E., there were three messianic pretenders, Judas the

Galilean, Simon, and Athronges. At the beginning of his public ministry, he was baptized by John the Baptizer, who, in the hallowed tradition of apocalyptic prophets, radically condemned the established order of Israel, called for national repentance to prepare for the imminent arrival of the Coming One, and indeed apparently hailed Jesus as that Coming One. Jesus' choice of the twelve disciples had the symbolic meaning of the renewal of the twelve tribes of Israel. His cleansing of the Temple was the prophetic symbol of its destruction and renewal. His miracles were signs that the new world was aborning. And, finally, his execution by the Roman authorities for sedition intimated that they perceived him as one of the apocalyptic revolutionaries.

Furthermore, with regard to his teaching, if there is anything certain about the earthly Jesus, it is that Jesus announced the kingdom or rule of God. Of the 122 times this expression is used in the New Testament, 99 appear in the Synoptic Gospels, and in 90 instances the phrase is put on the lips of Jesus.

There are some scholars (e.g., T. F. Glasson, Marcus J. Borg, and B. Mack) who would dispute that Jesus' outlook was shaped by Jewish apocalypticism and would argue that Jesus was a Cynic sage rather than a messianic preacher. The great majority of biblical scholars, however, would hold that Jesus stood squarely within the apocalyptic tradition. They point out that the movement with which he associated himself, that of John the Baptizer, was apocalyptic. Furthermore, the movement that issued from him immediately after his death, the earliest Christian community in Jerusalem, interpreted him both as the expected Messiah and the Son of Man and was itself also apocalyptic.

Q. 21. Did Jesus believe that the end-time would come soon?

As to what Jesus thought about the time of the coming of the kingdom of God, scholars are divided. In general there are three positions. First, some (e.g., Johannes Weiss, Albert Schweitzer, F. C. Burkitt, Martin Dibelius, Rudolf Bultmann, and R. H. Hiers) hold that Jesus believed that the kingdom of God that he announced was a completely *future* reality (*consistent* eschatology). For Schweitzer in particular, Jesus predicted the imminent coming of the Son of Man and the sufferings of his disciples. Both predictions did not come about, and so

Jesus decided to undergo death himself in an attempt to force the arrival of the kingdom of God. In Schweitzer's estimation, Jesus was an example of a failed apocalypticist.

Second, others (e.g., Charles Dodd) proposed that for Jesus the kingdom was an essentially *present* reality (*realized* eschatology). This view is defended principally on the basis of the parables, the Gospel of John, and Hebrews.

Third, others (e.g., Joachim Jeremias, Oscar Cullmann, and W. G. Kümmel) hold that there is a tension in Jesus' understanding of the kingdom of God. For Jesus it is *both* a present reality and a future expectation. It is a future reality that will appear imminently and is present in and through the words and deeds of Jesus. There are both an *already* and a *not-yet* in Jesus' proclamation of the kingdom of God (*proleptic* or *inaugurated* eschatology). For Kümmel, Jesus' teaching on the presence of the kingdom of God should be contrasted with that of the earlier Jewish apocalypticists insofar as for Jesus the future judgment and salvation were not mere future events but already present realities in his person and mission.

In sum, in the Judaism of the time of Jesus, there was a widespread expectation that God would soon act in a decisive way to redeem God's people. In view of Jesus' sayings and actions, the third position seems to reflect most accurately Jesus' mind. In many sayings and parables (e.g., Mt 11:5–6; 12:28; 13:16–17; 18:23–25; 20:1–6; Lk 4:16–30; 7:22–23; 17:20–21) Jesus is depicted as announcing the presence of the kingdom of God. On the other hand, in many other sayings and parables (e.g., Mt 5:3–12; 6:9–13; 8:11–12; Mk 9:1; Lk 9:27) the future arrival of the kingdom of God is emphasized. Thus, the overwhelming evidence suggests that Jesus understood that the kingdom of God was provisionally present in his own person and message and that its complete arrival also lay in an imminent future.

Q. 22. You mentioned above that Jesus' immediate followers formed an apocalyptic movement. What did Paul say about eschatology?

I will expound their specific teachings on eschatological themes in the following chapters. Here suffice it to highlight the intensely eschatological orientation of the early Christian community. That apocalyptic eschatology was the framework in which Paul formulated his gospel is clearly demonstrated in 1 Thessalonians 1:9–10 where he relates how the Thessalonians "turned to God from idols to serve the living and true God and to await his Son from heaven, whom he raised from [the] dead, Jesus, who delivers us from the coming wrath." Here Paul weaves together the themes of resurrection, parousia (Jesus' second coming), and universal judgment to characterize the beliefs of the early Christians.

Characteristic of Pauline eschatology is the dualistic separation between this present age and the coming age (*temporal* dualism) and between the age that is our world, full of evil powers, and the age that is a heavenly reality (*spatial* dualism). Because of his faith in Jesus' resurrection, Paul modifies the Jewish apocalyptic conception of the two ages: for him, the future age had already begun because Jesus' resurrection is the "firstfruits of those who have fallen asleep" (1 Cor 15:20), the first stage in the future resurrection of all the righteous dead.

As a consequence, Christians can experience the future age in the present age (1 Cor 2:6; 7:29–31). Of course, this experience, though real, is only a foretaste of what is still to come, and the full transformation of the Christians and the cosmos will not be realized until the parousia of Jesus (1 Thes 4; 1 Cor 15:51–56; Phil 3:20 f.). By virtue of his faith in Jesus, Paul also shifted the center of eschatology from God to Christ; the "day of Yahweh" becomes the "day of our Lord Jesus" (1 (1 Cor 1:8).

Also distinctive of Paul's eschatology is his belief in the imminence of the end. At times Paul clearly expected to be still alive at Christ's return from heaven (1 Thes 4:15, 17; 1 Cor 15:15–52). Elsewhere he reckoned with the possibility that he, as well as others, may die before the parousia. He expects that immediately after death the faithful will enjoy at least some of the benefits of salvation, such as union with Christ (Phil 1:23) and the gift of a "spiritual body" (1 Cor 15:44).

The tension between these two sets of statements may be explained by the two perspectives in which affirmations about the end-time can be made. From the *temporal* point of view, the end-time is still a future reality; hence, one may not be alive when it arrives and must look forward to it in hope. On the other hand, from the *spatial* perspective, the future heavenly world is already here; it is the world in which Christians live, and one may expect that it will come fully before one's death.

Further, another trademark of Paul's eschatology is the belief that the anticipated victory of God in the end-time affects not only individuals and the human race but also the cosmos. Paul declares that "creation awaits with eager expectation the revelation of the children of God…in hope that creation itself would be set free from slavery to corruption and share in the glorious freedom of the children of God. We know that all creation is groaning in labor pains even until now; and not only that, but we ourselves, who have the firstfruits of the Spirit, we also groan within ourselves as we wait for adoption, the redemption of our bodies" (Rom 8:19–23).

Finally, for Paul, eschatology is no abstract speculation on the other side. It has practical implications for ethics. He often uses eschatological language to urge good behavior. In Galatians 5:21, where, after listing a series of unacceptable acts, he warns that "those who do such things will not inherit the kingdom of God." Here the eschatological reality is used as a direct sanction against certain types of immoral behavior.

Q. 23. What do the Synoptic Gospels say about eschatology?

Before surveying the Synoptic Gospels, a few words should be said about the so-called Q (from the German *Quelle,* meaning source), that is, the some 250 verses common to Matthew and Luke but not found in Mark. There is a strong and pervasive emphasis on eschatology in Q. It expresses an intense expectation of the imminent end, connected with threats of judgment by the soon-to-come judge. Of the nine Son of Man sayings in Q, six focus on the future coming of the Son of Man (Lk 11:30 = Mt 12:40; Lk 12:40 = Mt 24:44; Lk 12:8–9 = Mt 10:32–33; Lk 17:24 = Mt 24:27; Lk 17:26 = Mt 24:37–39; Lk 17:28 = Mt 24:37–39), and three describe his present activity (Lk 7:34 = Mt 11:19; Lk 12:10 = Mt 12:32; Lk 9:58 = Mt 8:20).

Mark makes the "kingdom of God" the basic theme of Jesus' preaching: "This is the time of fulfillment. The kingdom of God is at hand. Repent, and believe in the gospel" (Mk 1:15). The kingdom of

God (the expression occurs fourteen times in Mark) is a future, imminent reality. As far as eschatology is concerned, Mark 13 is the most significant chapter. After predicting the destruction of the Temple, Jesus gives a series of signs of the end-time. After a cosmic upheaval, the Son of Man will come in the clouds and gather his elect from all parts of the world.

Matthew uses the expression "kingdom of heaven" (a pious circumlocution for "kingdom of God") thirty-two times, "kingdom of God" four times, and "kingdom" in conjunction with other modifiers fourteen times. For Matthew, in his life and ministry Jesus fulfilled all the eschatological promises God made in the Old Testament, and the church is the true Israel. With regard to eschatology, chapters 24–25 are the most important. There we find the destruction of the Temple foretold, the signs of the end-time enumerated, and the coming of the Son of Man for judgment announced. Matthew emphasizes the theme of eschatological judgment by adding several parables (the ten virgins, the talents, the last judgment) and the duty of vigilance. Matthew is the first author to use the Greek term *parousia* in the technical sense of the second coming of Christ (24:3; 14:27, 37, 39).

Luke relates Jesus' response to the Pharisees' question about the time of the coming of God's kingdom with the claim that "the coming of the kingdom of God cannot be observed" (17:20). But Jesus goes on to affirm that "the kingdom of God is among you" (17:21). The shift is therefore made from an imminent coming of the kingdom observable by means of external signs to something that is already present in Jesus' person and ministry.

Luke does have an eschatological discourse parallel to Mark 13 and Matthew 24–25 in chapter 21, but he has made important changes to the words of Jesus found there. Whereas Mark describes the desecration of the Jerusalem Temple by the Romans in 70 C.E. (the "desolating abomination") as an apocalyptic symbol accompanying the end of the age and the coming of the Son of Man, Luke (21:20–24) removes the apocalyptic setting and separates the historical destruction of Jerusalem from the signs of the coming of the Son of Man by a period he refers to as "the times of the Gentiles" (21:24). In so doing, Luke attempts to come to terms with the community's experience of what has been called the "delay of the parousia," which was supposed to happen soon after the destruction of Jerusalem. By temporally separating the two events, Luke wishes to preserve the sense of anticipation of the end-time and encourage vigilance for it, while responding to the problem of why the parousia did not come about as expected.

Q. 24. What does the Gospel of John say about eschatology?

If Mark is most oriented to the future, John is most oriented to the present. No wonder that John is most often invoked to defend realized eschatology. Of course, the future dimension is not forgotten: there is mention of the future resurrection "on the last day" (5:28–29; 6:39, 40, 44, 54); of the second coming (14:3, 18; 21:21–23); and of a future judgment on "the last day" (12:48). However, for the Fourth Gospel, the eschatological judgment of God has already occurred in the sending of God's only Son into the world and in the human response to him. The benefits of the future salvation are already experienced by the Johannine community in four major ways: (1) the gift of the Spirit-Paraclete, (2) the possession of eternal life, (3) the divine judgment, and (4) the presence of Jesus as the Messiah.

Q. 25. The Book of Revelation has been used by many people to describe what will happen at the end of the world. What does it say about eschatology?

As pointed out above, Revelation 1:1–3 virtually defines apocalypse as a literary genre. No wonder, then, that in the history of Christianity, it has been used and much abused as a sourcebook for predictions about the end-time and what will happen in the beyond. To understand Revelation and what it says about eschatology correctly, it is vital to remember what we said about the process of interpretation in the last chapter and about the apocalyptic genre above.

As a typical piece of apocalyptic literature (except the fact that it is not pseudonymous), Revelation provides a limitless resource for crystal ball gazers with its numerous visions, angels, beasts, numbers, the antichrist, cosmic catastrophes, and the Armageddon. Candidates to incarnate the beast with the number 666 (Rv 13:18) have ranged from

Nero to Saddam Hussein, and the Armageddon has been identified as either of the two world wars and the Gulf War.

As a matter of fact, however, these scenarios are not intended as journalistic descriptions of historical events to be taken literally. Rather, they are stock-in-trade features of symbolic and imaginative constructions used by apocalyptic literature to make its basic point: despite appearances to the contrary suggested by oppression and persecution of God's faithful ones by the impious, God controls the course of history and will definitively triumph over the impious, and God's people will share in this victory.

Probably written during the persecutions of Christians by Roman emperors, Revelation is a sequential narrative of future events that is similar to the eschatological scenarios given in Mark 13, Matthew 24–25, Luke 21, 1 Thessalonians 4:13–18, and 2 Thessalonians 2:1–12 mentioned above. In this narrative the enemies of God's people are punished; Babylon-Rome is destroyed; and Christ is depicted as a field marshal leading the heavenly armies in a decisive combat with his enemies, natural and supernatural. Satan's defeat ushers in a kingdom over which Christ and his resurrected saints will reign for a thousand years, followed by the final battle and punishment of Satan and his allies. Then come the general resurrection of all the dead and the judgment by Christ. After the destruction of the first heaven and earth, a new heaven and earth are created, and the heavenly Jerusalem descends from heaven to earth, ushering in the new age.

Revelation is filled with a sense of urgency and expectation. Christ reiterates his promise that he will come *soon,* to which the faithful cry out, "Amen! Come, Lord Jesus!" (22:20). Because of this firm faith in Jesus' future coming and final victory that Revelation inspires, it will remain a permanently powerful voice to which Christians, especially in trying times, will heed.

Q. 26. You have repeatedly emphasized the importance of paying attention to the literary devices in interpreting apocalyptic scenarios given by both the Old and New Testaments. Could you give a list of these?

At the end of this exposition on biblical eschatology, it may be helpful to collate together the various images used by eschatological/

apocalyptic literature to depict the end-time and the beyond. While the list is not exhaustive, it includes the following: for prophetic eschatology—natural disasters, desecration of the Temple, profanation of the cult, loss of monarchy and priesthood, exile from the land, oppression of all kinds; for Hebrew apocalyptic eschatology—pseudonymity, the two-age dualism, visions, dreams, otherworldly journeys, angels, secret scrolls; and for New Testament eschatology/apocalypsis—destruction of the Jerusalem Temple, wars, famines, earthquakes, persecutions, false prophecies, worldwide preaching of the gospel, appearance of the antichrist, hatred among family members, the increase of evil, the darkening of the sun and the moon, the falling of stars, the coming of the Son of Man on the clouds, angels with trumpet blasts, the gathering of all the faithful, the resurrection of the dead, the judgment of the nations.

The final victory is described in various images: for Old Testament prophetic eschatology—a new creation, a new exodus, a new covenant, restoration of the Davidic dynasty, rebuilding of Jerusalem, reconsecration of the Temple, restoration of the cult, reunification of the nation, total faithfulness to the Torah; for apocalyptic eschatology—destruction of the old age and of this world, punishment of the enemies of God's people, victory of the faithful, enthronment of Yahweh; and for the New Testament—the parousia, the punishment of Satan and his cohorts, the millennial reign, the victory of Christ, the new heaven and the new earth, the heavenly Jerusalem.

It is by navigating carefully this deep and treacherous sea of symbolism that we can derive the teaching of the Bible about the afterlife for our times. In so doing, one may take as useful guides four principles proposed by Zachary Hayes:

1. The norm for Christian eschatology is the life, teaching, death, and resurrection of Jesus Christ. In light of this norm, we have to deal with both the individual and collective dimensions of eschatology as well as the bodily and spiritual aspects of human existence.

2. Both the present and future dimensions of eschatology must be maintained. Although in and through grace we truly and really experience the future glory in the present, nevertheless, there remains a future fulfillment of our existence and the cosmos that is an object of hope.

3. Although apocalypticism had a profound influence on Christianity, Christianity is not reducible to it.

4. Christian eschatology with its vision of a transcendent future is ultimately a mystery and therefore must be differentiated from a false apocalypticism (which is often fundamentalistic), whose aim is to find every correspondence between apocalyptic predictions and past or current events and persons and whose tendency is to speculate on the details of the end-time (*Visions of a Future*, 66–67).

One can perhaps expand the last point by saying with Karl Rahner that genuine eschatology focuses upon the *present* situation of grace and salvation and reads forward or extrapolates it into the future by asking how this present situation will be fulfilled in the light of what has happened to Christ. On the contrary, false eschatology focuses on the predictions about the *future* as realistic descriptions and reads backwards or interpolates them back into the present by asking what event or person in history corresponds to those predictions (*Theological Investigations*, 4:337). In other words, true eschatology is Christology and anthropology conjugated in the future tense.

CHAPTER III
DEATH AND DYING:
TIME MADE ETERNITY

Q. 27. You have mentioned reports on near-death experiences as one of the factors contributing to the recent interest in the afterlife. What are near-death experiences? What do they say about the afterlife?

With the publication of Raymond Moody's book *Life After Life* (1975) and the works of Dr. Elisabeth Kübler-Ross, widespread interest was aroused in near-death experiences (NDE). People who had been almost dead or declared clinically dead and who revived reported the following typical experiences: being aware that they were dead, leaving their bodies and looking down at them, entering a tunnel, seeing a light, meeting their loved ones and supernatural beings, seeing beautiful scenery, participating in the evaluation of their lives, reentering their bodies, experiencing joy and peace, and losing the fear of death.

To understand NDE properly, an important distinction must be made between *clinical* or reversible death in which external life signs such as consciousness, pulse, and breathing are absent (indicated by a flat EKG reading), followed by an absence of brain-wave activity (indicated by a flat EEG reading), and *physical* or irreversible death, which would always result if no steps are taken to reverse the process. Of course, reported NDE did not occur in biological death but only in cases of clinical death where there was confirmed heart stoppage (flat EKG) and even where there was no brain activity (flat EEG).

For some authors, for example, Gary R. Habermas and J. P. Moreland (*Immortality: The Other Side of Death,* 73–86), these conscious experiences after clinical death are convincing proof that there is at least some minimal life after death, especially after a prolonged period of flat EEG. For example, one woman, about three and one-half hours after she had been declared clinically dead because of flat EKG and EEG, revived and recounted in detail her experiences and even described accurately the designs of the doctors' ties! For others, for example, Hans Küng (*Eternal Life?* 14–20) and Zachary Hayes (*Visions of a Future,* 104), NDE are not proof that there is life beyond death, precisely because they are only *near-death* experiences.

Obviously, for those who already believe that there is the after-life, NDE provide a welcome confirmation for their belief. On the other hand, those who are philosophically opposed to the notion of immortality regard accounts of NDE as nothing more than psychological or cultural expressions of the wish for survival beyond the grave. In my judgment, NDE are not convincing proofs for the existence of the afterlife but are suggestive pointers for the possibility of the afterlife, the existence of which must be established on philosophical and theological grounds. Whatever the evidentiary value of NDE for the afterlife, there is no doubt that they are quite common and have a profound positive impact on those who have had them.

Q. 28. What does the Old Testament say about death and dying?

It is interesting that whereas Israel's neighbors (e.g., the Egyptians) practiced elaborate rituals to fend off the panoply of demons, ghosts, and gods associated with death, the ancient Hebrews regarded death rather matter-of-factly as the normal end of life, especially if it comes to one with sufficient progeny and old age (Gn 25:8). Human beings "perish like the beasts" (Ps 49:12). Death only becomes a problem when it is premature and when the focus shifts from the survival of the covenanted nation as a whole in its relationship with God to that of the individual whose death seems to terminate that relationship. This led to the psalmists' rejection of the finality of death and their affirmation of God's power extending beyond death (Pss 16; 49; 73).

Rather than discussing the nature of death and dying, the Old Testament is more interested in its cause: How did death first come about?

The answer given in Genesis 2–3 is that death is the punishment for disobeying God. Death as punishment for sin, however, does not consist so much in the cessation of physical life (which, as we have seen, is in a sense normal) as in the inability to praise God after death. Praising God is a sign of life; inability to do so is death, even in life. Clearly, then, the Old Testament views death not simply as a physical act (i.e., cessation of life) but also as a punishment for sin.

Q. 29. Does the Old Testament teach anything about life beyond death?

In my response to question 14, I have said that in the Old Testament no hope of individual survival after death is expressed except in some late texts probably written in the second century B.C.E. Here I would like to expand that statement. For the Hebrews, death affects the entire person as an indissoluble unity of body and spirit. There was no concept of a separate principle in the human person, for example, the soul, that is freed from the shackles of the body at death and survives apart from the body. After death, the entire person descends into Sheol, the dark abode of the dead, the underworld (often rendered as "hell," "grave," or "pit").

On the other hand, at death a person is not simply annihilated. The dead, apparently both righteous and wicked, go down into Sheol where they continue to exist. Such an existence, however, is not life since it is not possible to praise God there, and the person is cut off from God. It is like sleep or rest.

Eventually, however, the question of the ultimate vindication of the righteous began to emerge, for example, in Job and Ecclesiastes, where it is pointed out that the just do not always get what they deserve in this life. Gradually, ideas about a postmortem retribution were formed, based upon the belief in God as the source of life, the affirmation of God's justice, and an obscure presentiment of human immortality as indicated in the desire for permanence in progeny and good name. Metaphors of resurrection were used (e.g., Hos 6:1–2; Ez 37; and Is 24–27). Hosea predicts that God "will revive us after two days; on the third day he will raise us up, to live in his presence." Ezekiel presents a grandiose vision of scattered bones brought back to life by the breath of

God, symbolizing the rebirth of the Israelite nation. Isaiah says to the people, "Your dead shall live, their corpses shall rise;/awake and sing, you who lie in the dust" (26:19). These three texts may still have to be taken not as unambiguous affirmations of the afterlife but as metaphors for the faith in God as the supreme source of life who is never tired of coming to rescue God's people in their tribulations.

It is only with Daniel 12:1–3 that we have the first undisputed evidence of a belief in the resurrection. As mentioned in my answer to question 18, this text was written during the persecution by Antiochus IV Epiphanes (175–164 B.C.E.). The text refers to the resurrection of the members of the chosen people and of them alone, the just to eternal life (the first occurrence of this expression in the Bible), the others to everlasting shame. The problem of the suffering and persecuted righteous emerged in acute form and acted as a catalyst for the belief in the resurrection as vindication by God. Furthermore, according to Daniel 12:3, the wise teachers of the community, who have encouraged many to follow the path of righteousness, will receive special honor by being gloriously exalted among the stars and the angelic host.

Two other texts, which belong to the Christian Old Testament but not to the Hebrew Bible, affirm a belief in the future life when the just will find happiness with God. The Second Book of Maccabees, written in Greek in the latter part of the second century B.C.E., affirms, through the story of the martyrdom of seven young men and their mother, the resurrection of the just on the last day (7:9, 11, 14, 23; 14:46). Condemned to death by a human court (i.e., Antiochus IV Epiphanes), they await vindication by the supreme court of God. Bodily resurrection by God is the response to bodily destruction by the wicked. Furthermore, 2 Maccabees affirms the intercession of the saints in heaven for those living on earth, and the power of the living to offer prayers and sacrifices for the dead (12:39–46).

The Book of Wisdom, also written in Greek in Alexandria in the first century B.C.E., betrays the influence of Hellenistic thought. Here (1:11; 3:1), for the first time, the concept of *psyche* (soul) was introduced to refer to the immortal spiritual principle in the human person as opposed to the perishable material body, even though the book nowhere uses the phrase "immortal soul." Furthermore, "immortality" (3:4; 4:1; 8:13, 17; 15:3) and "incorruptibility" (2:23; 6:18) are not presented as natural qualities of human nature but as God's gift to the righteous and the fruits of union with wisdom (6:18; 8:13, 17; 15:3). Finally, the book reinterprets Genesis 3 by claiming that it was the devil's envy that brought death into the world (2:24).

In sum, there is a development in the Old Testament regarding the life beyond death, from a belief in a postmortem shadowy existence in the underworld to the affirmation of the resurrection of the dead, at least of the just. At any rate, by the time of the New Testament, there were four positions regarding life beyond death. (1) The Sadducees believed that with death the person is totally destroyed. (2) The Pharisees affirmed bodily resurrection on the last day. (3) The Essenes taught the immortality of the soul. (4) The Qumran community appeared to hold that there will not be a bodily resurrection; rather, there will be a mode of existence like that of the angels in heaven.

Q. 30. What does the New Testament say about death?

Much of what the New Testament authors say about death and dying is derived from their Jewish background but reinterpreted in the light of Jesus' death and resurrection. Thus, death for humans is universal (Heb 9:27), except for Enoch (Gn 5:24; Heb 11:5) and Elijah (2 Kgs 2:11). It is affirmed that God alone is immortal (1 Tm 6:16).

Though universal, death, at least as a threat of a painful and dreaded destruction of the self, is not part of God's original plan for the human race but a penalty for sin. "The wages of sin is death" (Rom 6:23). "Through one person sin entered the world, and through sin, death, and thus death came to all, inasmuch as all sinned" (Rom 5:12).

However, just as sin and death came to the human race through one man, Adam, so with the death and resurrection of one man, Christ, the new Adam, says Paul, acquittal, grace, and eternal life came to all in much greater measure (Rom 5:12–21). So Christ's death destroyed "the one who has the power of death, that is, the devil" (Heb 2:14); indeed, by dying Christ destroyed death itself (2 Tm 1:10), "the last enemy" to be conquered (1 Cor 15:26). Death could not hold Christ (Acts 2:24), so now Christ is "Lord of both the dead and the living" (Rom 14:9) and holds "the keys to death and the netherworld" (Rv 1:18).

As I said in my answer to question 12, Christ is both the cause and model of our eternal life. In light of this principle, death is itself viewed in the light of Jesus' resurrection. This is clear from the fact that in the seventy-five places where the word *nekros* (the dead) is used in the New Testament, it is the object of the verb *egeiro* (to awaken) or *anastasis* (to raise). Christ is said to be the first person raised from the dead (Col 1:18; Rv 1:5). Because of Christ's death and resurrection, death now acquires a positive meaning. Without losing its terror, death may now appear as a "gain" (Phil 1:21); indeed, the Christian, like Paul, may even desire death: "I long to depart this life and be with Christ" (Phil 1:23).

Q. 31. In death, what happens to me? Can it be said that my soul is separated from my body?

Christian Tradition has often described death as separation of the soul from the body. The *Catechism of the Catholic Church* still uses this language (see nos. 1005, 1016). Just as any theological language, this expression is rooted in a certain interpretation of reality, in this case Platonic philosophy. Plato (ca. 427–347 B.C.E.) teaches that as spirit is opposed to matter, so the human soul is hostile to the body and is forced to be united to it. So, at death, the soul is freed from the body as from fetters or prison. If the soul and the body are conceived in this fashion (and there is no denying that Platonic philosophy has exercised a profound influence on Christian theology), then the definition of death as "separation of the soul from the body" is extremely misleading and anti-Christian.

On the other hand, if the human person is understood as intrinsically *one* reality, then this definition powerfully highlights one of the reasons why death strikes terror in the human heart, as Ernest Becker describes so well in his book *The Denial of Death:* death is the dissolution of the very human person, and not just the body. It is not just the body that dies, it is *I* who die. As the International Theological Commission puts it, "death intrinsically tears people asunder. Indeed, since the person is not the soul alone, but the body and soul essentially united, death affects the person" ("Some Current Questions in Eschatology," 226).

One way of explaining the essential unity of the human person has been to borrow the philosophy of the Greek philosopher Aristotle (ca. 384–322 B.C.E.) on the soul and at the same time to modify it to preserve the Christian teaching on the afterlife. For Aristotle, the soul is the *form* of the body, an intrinsic element of the human person, and cannot exist apart from the body, just as the body cannot exist except as *informed* by the soul. Aristotle did not envisage the possibility of the survival of the human person after death in any way. Thomas Aquinas (1225–74), in contrast to Aristotle, held that though the soul has an intrinsic orientation toward matter, after death it can exist for a time without that orientation being actually realized until it is eventually reunited with the body at the resurrection. This is what is called the "separated soul."

In sum, the traditional description of death as separation of the soul from the body is correct as long as it is used to maintain two important truths, namely, that death affects the entire person and that one constitutive element of the human person called "soul" survives death (immortality of the soul).

Q. 32. Besides this way of describing death, is there any other way that is coherent with the Christian faith?

In one of his books, *On the Theology of Death,* Karl Rahner points out that one of the inadequacies of the traditional description of death is that it does not differentiate the death of the human person from that of a plant or an animal. A plant or an animal simply perishes, whereas humans die, being spiritual and free persons. A beast dies less of a death than a human being. Of course, Rahner does not deny that death is a physical act that *happens* to a person, a fate imposed from the outside, something that is, in Tony Kelly's powerful language, "final, alien and violent, dark, silent, ugly, obscene, repulsive" (*Touching on the Infinite,* 68–69). Death in this sense is an act of a man or woman as *nature,* something a human being suffers.

On the other hand, as I pointed out in my answer to question 10, because they are endowed with freedom, human beings are able to choose this or that option. More importantly, however, in and through these choices, they shape their identity and destiny in a definitive and decisive way. For Rahner, dying, a process that may include near-death experiences, is the act whereby a person freely gathers up or consummates his or her history of freedom in a final and definitive way. Of course, this gathering up occurs throughout one's life, in the many significant choices one makes in freedom, whereby one's past, present, and future are gathered into a unity. But dying, which is the person's last act, is the act par excellence by which a person determines his or her destiny, *finally, definitively, irrevocably.* Death in this sense is an act of a man or a woman as *person,* something the human being performs in freedom. In dying the person brings to a definitive end all that he or she has accomplished throughout his or her life. Dying is the privileged moment of human freedom in which the person has the power to make a decision that is of eternal validity. In its totality, death is thus both an act of nature and an act of the person, a passion and an action, destruction and self-possession.

There is another aspect to dying and death that must be highlighted. Just as the person is essentially *interpersonal,* that is, constituted by relations, so dying, which is the most personal act, is also interpersonal. In death one loses not only biological life but also, and above all, the network of relationships and structures of meaning that nourish one's physical and spiritual life. That is why it is vital that all care should be taken that a person die not in loneliness but surrounded as far as possible by all his or her loved ones and accompanied by their support and prayers. In this sense immortality is not just the survival of an individual soul apart from its body but the continued existence of the person amidst all the myriad relationships that have formed and nurtured him or her throughout life.

Q. 33. I can easily understand how death is something that is forced upon me. But how does one act or perform one's dying in freedom?

One acts or performs dying in one's attitude toward death throughout one's life and, supremely, in the moment of dying. In the face of death, one can adopt either of the following two postures. One is to run away from it, to deny it existentially by trying to achieve immortality through progeny, fame, power, and myriad activities. As Ernest Becker puts it, "the idea of death, the fear of it, haunts the human animal like nothing else; it is the mainspring of human activity—activity designed largely to avoid the fatality of death, to overcome it by denying in some way that it is the final destiny for man" (*The Denial of Death,* ix).

The other posture is to accept, freely and willingly, one's own mortality, with all that this implies in terms of limitation and finitude, as a unique opportunity to realize oneself definitively and irrevocably through freedom, as the light that illumines everything of one's existence. Such an acceptance is no mere intellectual assent to the abstract proposition that one will die. Rather, it is embodied in a spirituality or way of living marked by gratitude for the gift of life, seriousness about the responsibility of shaping one's destiny through freedom, acceptance of one's limitations and weaknesses, and humble courage in the face of sickness, old age, and ultimately death.

The Christian may even *desire* death, not in order to avoid suffering, but as the path to union with the risen Christ, as Paul did (Phil 1:23), and to a deeper immersion in the mystery of God. This *death mysticism,* of course, does not dispense Christians from taking good care of their bodies and does not give them the right to take positive steps to hasten their own death.

Perhaps the best example of this mysticism is found in Francis of Assisi's Canticle of the Creatures in which the Poverello gives thanks to God not only for the gift of life but also for the fate of death:

> Praised are you, my Lord, for our sister bodily Death,
> from whom no living person can escape.
> Woe to those who will die in mortal sin!
> Blessed are they who will be found
> in your most holy will,
> for the second death will not harm them.

Q. 34. How can I prepare myself for death?

One does not prepare for death just in the last few minutes or days of one's life on the deathbed or at the onset of an incurable disease. Of course, these times are of great significance, and the church, as we shall see below, surrounds them with particular rituals and prayers. For the Christian, preparing for death is a lifelong task, since one truly dies in every moment of one's life. This task is begun in baptism, in which the Christian dies, is buried, and rises sacramentally with Christ. This death, which is a participation in Christ's death, is a death to sin, and since physical death is a punishment for sin, dying to sin is already a preparation for and overcoming of physical death. This journey from death to life is sustained also by the other sacraments—supremely by the Eucharist—which deepen the Christian's companionship with Christ in suffering and death.

Sickness and old age are moments in which the threat of death is made more immediate. The church shows its solicitude and love for the sick and the aged by surrounding them with manifold rituals. It encourages pastoral visits to the aged and those in poor health; it urges that the sick and the aged be given the opportunity to receive the Eucharist frequently and that those in danger of death be given the viaticum; it celebrates the sacraments of reconciliation and anointing of the sick for them; and it performs the rite of the commendation of the dying for those in agony.

The departing Christian consummates his or her life, bringing his or her history of freedom to a definitive end, fortified by the church's prayer:

> My brother (sister) in faith, I entrust you to God who created you. May you return to the one who formed you from the dust of this earth. May Mary, the angels, and all the saints come to meet you as you go forth from this life. May Christ who was crucified for you bring you freedom and peace. May Christ, the Son of God, who died for you, take you into his kingdom. May Christ, the Good Shepherd, give you a place in his flock. May he forgive your sins and keep you among his people. May you see your Redeemer face to face and enjoy the sight of God for ever. Amen. ("Rite for the Commendation of the Dying," in The Rites of the Catholic Church, 625–260)

Of course, the Christian's preparation for death is not limited to sacramental celebrations; it includes the whole of life. Rahner summarizes this preparation well: "Christian vigilance, remembrance of the Last Things, waiting for the Lord, joy at his nearness, the groaning of the creation for redemption, for the glorification of the body as it perhaps begins even in this life, through a slow approach to the ideal of Paradise, of freedom from concupiscence by means of an ascetical life" (*On the Theology of Death*, 72).

Q. 35. If one prepares for death in this way, can we eliminate the fear of death?

Not necessarily. Faith and hope may lessen our fear of death, but they in no way remove it. Even when fortified by the sacraments and accompanied by the prayers of the community of faith, the Christian still performs the last act of his or her life in fear and trembling. Unlike Socrates, who drank the hemlock with philosophical equanimity, discoursing calmly on the immortality of the soul, Jesus faced his death in anguish, to the point of sweating blood, and implored his Father to remove the chalice if he so willed. On the cross he experienced death as radical loneliness and abandonment by God: "My God, my God, why have you forsaken me?" (Mk 15:34). But Jesus also performed his dying in a radical acceptance of and loving obedience to God in the midst of such emptiness and powerlessness: "Father, into your hands I commend my spirit" (Lk 23:46).

The Christian, too, who "dies in the Lord" (1 Thes 4:16; 1 Cor 15:18) undergoes that same conflicting experience of remoteness and nearness to God, doubt and faith, despair and hope, defiant rebellion and loving obedience. With God's grace, death, which is a penalty for sin, becomes an event of grace and salvation. Like Christ's death, our death can be the final act of self-surrender in faith, hope, and love, despite utter darkness, to that Mystery in whom we have trusted throughout our life and whom we have confessed to be a God of love, forgiveness, and acceptance. Death is the final extension of the lifelong risk of love.

Q. 36. Is cremation of the corpse permitted to Catholics?

Up to 1963 the burning of the corpse as a way of burial was strictly forbidden. The 1917 Code of Canon Law stated: "The bodies of the faithful departed must be buried and their cremation is reprobated" (c. 1203.1). If they had been cremated, their ashes could not be preserved in a blessed cemetery (the Holy Office, 19 June 1926). The church's opposition to cremation was motivated by the fear that cremation may deny faith in the resurrection and lessen reverence for the body as a member of Christ and temple of the Holy Spirit.

On 8 May 1963, the Holy Office modified the law forbidding cremation. Cremation had been permitted only for the disposal of bodies in time of pestilence, natural disaster, or other grave public necessity. Now it could be allowed for any sound reason, provided the request was not motivated by a denial of Christian dogmas and hatred of the Catholic Church.

The 1983 Code of Canon Law recommends burial but permits cremation, provided that it does not imply a denial of faith in the resurrection of the body (c. 1176.3). The *Catechism of the Catholic Church* teaches that we should treat the bodies of the dead with respect and love and reminds us that the burial of the dead is one of the corporal works of mercy (see no. 2300).

CHAPTER IV
FROM DEATH TO RESURRECTION:
THE INTERMEDIATE STATE

Q. 37. What happens to me immediately after I die?

It is important to recall a point repeatedly emphasized in the last chapter on the meaning of death, namely, that in dying we *definitively, irrevocably, irreversibly* decide our final destiny. The *Catechism of the Catholic Church* states: "Death is the end of the human person's earthly pilgrimage, of the time of grace and mercy which God offers him or her so as to work out the earthly life in keeping with the divine plan, and to decide his or her ultimate destiny" (no. 1012).

Death, then, is not merely cessation of physical life but primarily the end of *personal* history. Whatever awaits us after our death, it is not an endless continuation of our temporal existence in another world or entrance into another life similar to this one. Rather, with death we enter into eternity (see answers to questions 9 and 10), no longer able to make changes to the radical decision for or against God we have made throughout our life and finally in our dying.

Q. 38. Do you mean that there is no possibility of reincarnation?

The belief in reincarnation, recently made popular in the United States by the New Age movement, is the doctrine that the soul becomes incarnate in a succession of bodies until, by means of a complete purification, it is liberated from its bodily existence. This belief is widespread, especially in India. In Hinduism, for instance, it is believed that the soul is entrapped in the body and needs to be saved by escaping from the body into the *atman* (all-soul). However, because this process of liberation is too difficult to be accomplished in a lifetime, the individual is given as many chances (incarnations) as necessary to achieve this goal.

Accordingly, a human being is assigned to a social stratum (caste) to live out any one existence, and there is no upward mobility during that lifetime. How well an individual fulfills the socioreligious duties associated with that station in life *(dharma)* determines the next level, higher or lower, at which she or he will be reincarnated. The process of reward-punishment according to one's actions *(karma)* is inexorable. Throughout reincarnations, the physical body perishes, but the eternal, spiritual reality *(jiva),* in which a complete memory of the whole series of lives is preserved, is passed on to successive bodies until it reaches enlightenment *(moksha).* Then it becomes consciously one with the universal *atman,* or self, which is identical with Brahman, the eternal absolute Reality.

Buddhism, which rejects the Hindu concept of caste and teaches that there is no soul *(anatta)* and no permanent self *(anicca),* accepts a modified version of reincarnation. At death, the self, which is not a unified entity but simply an aggregation of "heaps" *(skandhas),* is dissolved into these components. But *karma,* that is, actions and their consequences, determines one's destiny, and karmic states (not the soul) that have not achieved enlightenment will be reborn as a god, a human being, an animal, a ghost, or a denizen of hell.

Supporters of reincarnation often cite as evidence the memories of those who claim to have lived another life at some earlier time, cases of individuals who can speak a language they do not know, the presence of birthmarks on the alleged reincarnated person that match with those of the deceased, and the agreement between the child's character and that of the deceased individual. Geddes MacGregor, an Anglican theologian, has even attempted to use biblical texts to support the doctrine of reincarnation in his *Reincarnation in Christianity.*

Those who are opposed to the doctrine claim that the alleged phenomenon of reincarnation could be explained by possession either by demons or by the spirit of the deceased person (e.g., Gary R. Habermas and J. P. Moreland, *Immortality: The Other Side of Death,* 123–26). Hans Küng, after carefully weighing the arguments for and against reincarnation, concludes: "...it cannot in any case be said that the doctrine of reincarnation has been proved. In fact, despite all its attractiveness, there are quite weighty arguments against the idea of rebirth which are not to be ignored: it is also notable that educated Indians, Chinese and Japanese often show considerable skepticism in regard to the idea of reincarnation" (*Eternal Life?* 64).

The teaching of the Catholic Church has been consistently opposed to reincarnation. The *Catechism of the Catholic Church* states that there is no reincarnation after death (see no. 1013). A recent document of the International Theological Commission argues that the doctrine of reincarnation is "a child of paganism in direct opposition to Scripture and Church tradition, and has been always rejected by Christian faith and theology" ("Some Current Questions in Eschatology," 232–33).

Some of the reasons for which the church rejects the doctrine of reincarnation are the following. First, it seems to deny the possibility of hell, because through successive reincarnations all human beings will eventually be saved. Second, it seems to deny the doctrine of redemption, because it says that it is through one's moral efforts, and not God's grace, that the individual is saved. Third, it seems to lessen the seriousness of human freedom, since one's decisions in this life can be always revised. Fourth, it appears to deny the resurrection, because the reincarnation does not involve one's original body.

Q. 39. Granted that there is no possibility of reincarnation, after my death do I go to heaven (or to hell, God forbid!) immediately, or do I have to wait until the end of time?

Your question brings up an interesting historical fact. At the fourth session of the Second General Council of Lyons in 1274, convened by Pope Gregory X with the intention of bringing about a reunion between the Latin and Greek churches, the profession of faith that Pope Clement IV had proposed to Emperor Michael VIII Palaeologus in 1267 was read. This preconciliar document, which was neither discussed nor promulgated by the council, contains two teachings on eschatology, one of which concerns purgatory, and the other of which contains a response to the question you have just asked.

The Greeks had denied the possibility of *immediate* beatific vision and held that it would begin only at the general resurrection. The so-called Profession of Faith of Michael Palaeologus, however, states: "As for the souls of those who, after having received holy baptism, have incurred no stain of sin whatsoever, and those souls who, after having contracted the stain of sin, have been cleansed, either while remaining still in their bodies or after having been divested of them..., they are received immediately *[mox]* into heaven. As for the souls of those who die in mortal sin or with original sin only, they go down immediately *[mox]* to hell *[infernum]*, to be punished however with different punishments" (*The Christian Faith*, 18).

In 1331, Pope John XXII (1249–1334), in a series of sermons preached in Paris, suggested that soon after death the blessed enjoy only the vision of Christ's glorified humanity, while their vision of the Blessed Trinity would be postponed until the last judgment. The following year he applied a similar gradual retribution to the damned. His teaching, supported by the Franciscans, was vigorously resisted by the Dominican masters of the University of Paris. John XXII himself had said that he would be ready to abandon his opinion if it were proved to be contrary to the faith of the church. He was able to retract his teaching on the eve of his death. His successor, Pope Benedict XII, issued a constitution, *Benedictus Deus*, in 1336 reaffirming the traditional teaching regarding the *immediate* retribution, either in heaven or in hell, after death, before the general resurrection and final judgment.

The same teaching was reaffirmed by the General Council of Florence in 1439, using the identical words of the Council of Lyons, in another (unsuccessful) attempt at reunion with the Greek Church. Today, most theologians would say that the dead enjoy eternal happiness with God or suffer separation from God immediately after death. Some of them would add that their happiness or condemnation will not be complete until the end of time at the general resurrection of the dead.

Q. 40. When we discussed biblical eschatology, it was shown that the Bible affirms a belief in life beyond death. It was also shown that the Bible affirms a future resurrection "on the last day" (e.g., Jn 6:39, 40, 44, 54) and judgment "on the last day" (e.g., Jn 12:48). Does this mean that there is an intervening time between my death and my resurrection, during which I am either enjoying eternal happiness with God or condemned in hell?

The intervening time you refer to is called the "intermediate state." This is the "time" in which the "separate souls" exist apart from their bodies, awaiting the resurrection. This is the way in which traditional eschatology describes the mode of existence of the soul after death. I put the word *time* in quotation marks since, strictly speaking, there is no longer time for those who have died and entered into eternity. Arguments in favor of such an intermediate state include the view that humans are composed of body and soul, as Matthew 10:28 implies: "Do not be afraid of those who kill the body but cannot kill the soul; rather, be afraid of the one who can destroy both soul and body in Gehenna." Such an anthropology would entail that the soul survives death and awaits "in the meantime" the resurrection, which is affirmed to be a future event, "on the last day."

A document from the Congregation of the Doctrine of the Faith, *The Reality of Life after Death* (1979), affirms that "a spiritual element survives and subsists after death, an element endowed with consciousness and will, so that the 'human self' subsists. To designate this element, the Church uses the word 'soul,' the accepted term in the usage of Scripture and Tradition" (no. 4). This is the text printed in *Osservatore Romano* (23 July 1979, 7–8). However, in the text printed in the official *Acta Apostolicae Sedis* (71 [1979]), there is added, after "so that the 'human self' subsists," the phrase "while lacking in the interim the complement of its body *[interim tamen complemento sui corporis carens]."*

It would seem that this phrase was added in order to reaffirm the belief in the intermediate state, while in the first text the question about the intermediate state was left open. However, the existence of the intermediate state has been vigorously defended by the previously mentioned recent document of the International Theological Commission, "Some Current Questions in Eschatology."

Q. 41. Still, I find it difficult to imagine what existence in the intermediate state is like. Could you tell me what contemporary theologians think about it?

From the magisterial documents, it is clear that the separated souls, to quote Pope Benedict XII's constitution *Benedictus Deus,* "before they take up their bodies again and before the general judgment, have been, are and will be with Christ in heaven, in the heavenly kingdom and paradise, joined to the company of the holy angels" (*The Christian Faith,* 685). These souls are said to enjoy the vision of God and are "truly blessed and have eternal life and rest." On the other hand, because they are still separated from the bodies of which they are the "forms" (see the answer to question 31), the separated souls live, according to Thomas Aquinas, in an "unnatural" existence. Recall that for Thomas the union of body and the human soul constitute the person. Thus, the soul separated from the body is not the person; it cannot think and act as it did in this life. Nor, strictly speaking, is the dead body, one may add, a body; rather, it is a "corpse" or "cadaver." Separation of body and soul, though inevitable, is not natural to either. So, writes Thomas, "it is evident that the soul is naturally united to the body, but is separated from it against its own nature and *per accidens.* Whence the soul, cut off from the body, while it is without the body, is imperfect" (*Super primam epistolam ad Corinthios,* c. 15, lectio 2, n. 924). Indeed, Thomas uses the incompleteness of the human soul separated from the body as an argument for the necessity of the resurrection.

Given this unnatural, imperfect condition of the separated soul, which is difficult to reconcile with the presumed perfect happiness of the saved person, some contemporary theologians, for example, Karl Rahner, would argue that the intermediate state is not a dogma but a conceptual framework used to formulate certain beliefs about the afterlife. Of course, magisterial declarations about the afterlife, such as the teachings of the Councils of Lyons and Florence and of Pope Benedict XII, *assumed* that there is the intermediate state. The question, however, is whether they *meant* to define the intermediate state as a doctrine of faith.

Some theologians hold that they did not; these teachings were expressly concerned with the immediacy of reward and punishment after death and not with the intermediate state. As Rahner opines:

Basically, I should like to postulate the following: it is by no means certain that the doctrine about the intermediate state is *anything more* than an intellectual framework, or way of thinking. So whatever it has to tell us (apart from statements about the commencement through death of the final form of the human person's history of freedom, and about the inclusion of the body in this final form) does not necessarily have to be part of Christian eschatology itself. We might put the matter differently and say: no one is in danger of defending a heresy if one maintains the view that the single and total perfecting of the human person in 'body' and 'soul' takes place immediately after death, that the resurrection of the flesh and the general judgment take place 'parallel' to the temporal history of the world; and that both coincide with the sum of the particular judgments of individual men and women. ("The Intermediate State," *Theological Investigations,* 17:14–15)

Q. 42. Even if the intermediate state were not a doctrine of faith, there is still the teaching that each individual person will be judged by God after death. What does the church teach about this "particular judgment"?

In the Old Testament God is often presented as "judge of all the world" (Gn 18:25) and, more generally, as the "just God" (Mal 2:17). As we have seen in chapter 2, the prophets and apocalypticists announced the "day of Yahweh" or the "day of judgment" on which God will judge both Israel and the nations. In the New Testament, Jesus' entire preaching pointed to an approaching judgment (Mk 1:15; 9:1), and it is said that Jesus himself will be the eschatological judge (Mt 7:22; 13:41; 16:27; 25:31–46). We will return to this theme of final judgment later on.

Here we are speaking about what has been called the "particular judgment" or the judgment of the individual immediately after death. Interestingly, nowhere in the Old Testament is there mention of a particular, final, and definitive judgment of the individual immediately after death by God. Divine judgment and retribution were seen mostly in terms of prosperity, longevity, and progeny in this world. As far as we can establish, the belief in the judgment of individuals after death was first attested in the apocryphal book of *First Enoch* in which the righteous are assured that the gates of heaven will be opened to them and that they will be companions of angels (chap. 104). Similarly, the New Testament nowhere teaches *explicitly* that there is a particular judgment of each individual after death. At most it can be said that such a judgment is *implied* by the belief that the individual's eternal destiny is determined by his or her actions.

Among the early Christian writers, Augustine (354–430) speaks explicitly of a judgment that awaits the soul as soon as it is separated from the body and distinguishes this judgment from the final judgment at the resurrection. The *Catechism of the Catholic Church* also affirms that there is a particular judgment at the moment of death which is followed immediately by entrance into heaven (after purification if necessary) or by damnation (see no. 1022).

Q. 43. How does this particular judgment take place?

Here we should be careful to avoid all sorts of popular depictions of the particular judgment as a trial in which prosecution and defense lawyers (i.e., Satan and his cohort on the one hand and the angels and saints on the other) appear before an impartial judge (i.e., God) to argue their case for or against the defendant (i.e., the deceased person) whose every thought and deed have been recorded in the "book of life." In some paintings, the soul's good and bad actions are placed on a scale, and if the sum of its misdeeds tips the balance, Satan gleefully pulls his victim down into the gaping fiery furnace.

Theologically, the particular judgment should be understood in the context of dying itself. As we have seen in the last chapter, for human beings dying is primarily a personal act in which an individual brings his or her history to a final, definitive, and irrevocable end. In this act of dying freely accepted, a person expresses a definitive position vis-à-vis God, a position that he or she has taken throughout life but that is now recapitulated and made irreversible in this last personal act of dying. In so doing the person "judges" himself or herself. Of course, we judge ourselves throughout our lives each time we search our conscience and evaluate our motives and behaviors. But in these judgments we may be deluded or blinded by passion and bias. In dying, however, such possibility of error and self-deception is no longer possible, because the person is brought face-to-face with God. Whatever decision the person makes vis-à-vis God, God ratifies it and in this way "judges" it. In this judgment God also makes clear to that person what she or he has done with her or his life and the corresponding eternal destiny.

Q. 44. If someone does not die in "mortal sin" but dies in "venial sin," what will happen to that person?

The answer to your question is implied in the doctrine of purgatory. The *Catechism of the Catholic Church* states: "All who die in God's grace and friendship, but still imperfectly purified, are indeed assured of their eternal salvation; but after death they undergo purification, so as to achieve the holiness necessary to enter the joy of heaven. The Church gives the name *Purgatory* to this final purification of the elect, which is entirely different from the punishment of the damned" (nos. 1030–31).

It is acknowledged that an *explicit* doctrine of purgatory is not found in the Bible. The two main texts that are often appealed to as evidence, namely, 2 Maccabees 12:38–46 and 1 Corinthians 3:11–15, are no longer considered by contemporary exegetes as probative. In 2 Maccabees, it is related that Judas took up a collection and sent it to Jerusalem to obtain an expiatory sacrifice for some of his slain soldiers who had been found wearing the forbidden amulets for protection. It is claimed that this "atonement for the dead that they might be freed from this sin" (12:46) seems to indicate a belief in purgatory. 1 Corinthians 3:11–15 affirms that the work of each person will come to light and "will be revealed with fire, and the fire [itself] will test the quality of each one's work. If the work stands that someone built upon the foundation, that person will receive a wage. But if someone's work is burned up, that one will suffer loss; the person will be saved, but only as through fire." This fire is thought to be the fire of purgatory. For two other New Testament texts that are also cited in support of the doctrine of purgatory, see Matthew 5:26 and 12:32.

While the doctrine of purgatory may not be explicitly found in biblical texts, it is certainly implicit in the church's practice of praying for the dead. Recall what was said regarding "the law of prayer establishes the law of belief" in the answer to question 13. In "The Profession of Faith of Michael Palaeologus" there is mentioned a connection between purgatory and the "acts of intercession *(suffragia)* of the living faithful, namely, the sacrifices of the Mass, prayers, alms and other works of piety" *(The Christian Faith,* 18). One may add indulgences to the list of the *suffragia.* This same connection was also made by the Councils of Florence and Trent.

A passage from the Council of Trent, which issued a decree on purgatory in 1563, deserves full citation because of its doctrinal balance and pastoral prudence:

> The Catholic Church, instructed by the Holy Spirit and in accordance with sacred Scripture and the ancient Tradition of the Fathers, has taught in the holy councils and most recently in this ecumenical council that there is a purgatory and that the souls detained there are helped by the acts of intercession *(suffragia)* of the faithful, and especially by the acceptable sacrifice of the altar. Therefore this holy council commands the bishops to strive diligently that the sound doctrine of purgatory, handed down by the Holy Fathers and the sacred councils, be believed by the faithful and that it be adhered to, taught and preached everywhere. But let the more difficult and subtle questions which do not make for edification and, for the most part, are not conducive to an increase of piety, be excluded from the popular sermons to uneducated people. Likewise they should not permit opinions that are doubtful and tainted with error to be spread and exposed. As for those things that belong to the realm of curiosity or superstition, or smack of dishonorable gain, they should forbid them as scandalous and injurious to the faithful *(The Christian Faith,* 687).

Q. 45. Is purgatory a place, and how long does a person have to be there?

In answering this question, we should avoid what the Council of Trent calls "things that belong to the realm of curiosity or superstition." Popularly, purgatory has been represented as a "place" somewhere between heaven and hell, and the duration of purgatory has been calculated with great care. Spanish Dominican theologian Dominic Soto (1494–1550) and Spanish Jesuit theologian Juan Maldonado (1533–83) ventured to opine that no one remains in purgatory longer than ten years! Church practice used to measure partial indulgences in exact numbers of days.

Contemporary theology prefers to speak of purgatory as a *process* rather than as a place (hence, *purification* rather than purgatory). Indeed, that is the language commonly used by the early church and the Eastern churches. It was not until the late twelfth century that purgatory was thought of as a place (see Jacques Le Goff, *The Birth of Purgatory*). Furthermore, this process of purification is conceived less in terms of juridical expiation or punishment for sins than as maturation and spiritual growth.

This maturation is described by Rahner as "a maturing process of the person, through which, though gradually, all the powers of the human person become slowly integrated into the basic decision of the free person" ("Remarks on the Theology of Indulgences," in *Theological Investigations,* 2:197). Human beings are a multileveled reality; when they return to God, the innermost center of their personhood can be made whole immediately by God's grace, but the healing process on the physical, psychological, and spiritual levels can also be a gradual and painful transformation. This process of maturation is what is called purgatory.

As to the "time" of purgatory, there are still theologians who hold to the notion of a state of longer or shorter "duration" (e.g., Edmund Fortman, *Everlasting Life After Death,* 138). The majority of theologians, however, realizing the difficulty of speaking of time after death, prefer to speak of purgatory as a process occurring in the moment of death through which the person encounters God in a most profound and decisive way. This encounter may be understood as our "purgatorial fire," a moment of self-cleansing and self-integration causing varying degrees of pain (see, e.g., Ladislaus Boros, *The Mystery of Death,* 135). Joseph Ratzinger rejects the quantification of purgatory in terms of long or short duration. Rather, he views purgatory as "the inwardly necessary process of transformation in which a person becomes capable of Christ, capable of God and thus capable of unity with the whole communion of saints" (*Eschatology: Death and Eternal Life,* 230).

In sum, purgatory is, as Australian theologian Tony Kelly puts it concisely, "a decisive encounter with Christ," "conformity to the Crucified," "a suffering born out of love," and "the entry into a truly compassionate existence" (*Touching on the Infinite,* 168–72).

Q. 46. I haven't heard anything about limbo lately. Is there such a thing?

You are quite right. No recent magisterial document, including the *Catechism of the Catholic Church,* mentions limbo. Traditionally, a distinction has been made between limbo of the Fathers and limbo of infants. The former referred to the place, comparable to Sheol, where those who died before Christ went and into which Christ descended after death to save them. The latter referred to a place for infants who die with original sin but without any personal sin. Because these infants have not personally sinned, they would not be condemned to hell (though Augustine believed they were). On the other hand, because of original sin, they could not be admitted into heaven. So, limbo was designed for them as a place where they are "naturally" happy, though deprived of the beatific vision of God. Since contemporary theology has found ways to account for the eternal salvation (or lack of it) for infants who die with original sin but without personal sins, limbo has outlived its purpose.

CHAPTER V
HEAVEN AND HELL:
WITH GOD OR AWAY FROM GOD

Q. 47. It has been said that immediately after death (or after necessary purification) a person enjoys eternal happiness or suffers eternal damnation. Is it true that heaven and hell are the only two options for us?

In a strict sense, the answer is affirmative, since the hypothesis of limbo is no longer necessary, and purgatory is only a transitory process. It is important, however, to dispel a common misconception that heaven and hell are two equal options for us to choose from, as if God had created two final destinations for our life journey. It is clear from the Scriptures that God's only will is that all be saved and none be damned. For example, we read in the Letter to Timothy: "This is good and pleasing to God our savior, who wills everyone to be saved and to come to the knowledge of the truth" (1 Tm 2:3–4). John's gospel offers another example: "And this is the will of the one who sent me, that I should not lose anything of what he gave me, but that I should raise it [on] the last day" (Jn 6:39).

Among contemporary theologians, Karl Rahner and Hans Urs von Balthasar have strongly insisted on the priority and triumph of God's grace over sin, of salvation over condemnation. Rahner argues that "on principle only *one* predestination will be spoken of in Christian eschatology. And it contains only *one* theme which is there on its behalf: the victory of grace in redemption consummated" (*Theological Investigations,* 4:340). Von Balthasar points out that there is an "asymmetry" between the possibility and reality of human sin and God's ever-greater grace and love (Theodramatik 4:246–7).

Hence, there is no parallel between statements about heaven and hell. One must speak about heaven as reality and about hell as *possibility*. Though the possibility of hell is real, first of all for me, then maybe for others, neither Scripture nor church Tradition has claimed that anyone in fact has been or will be forever lost, whereas the church has declared certain people to have been definitively saved and has proposed them for our veneration (canonization). This is why in eschatology we speak of heaven as the destiny God wills for all and of hell only as the human person's rejection of heaven.

Q. 48. What does the Bible say about heaven as the eternal destiny of the just?

Imagination touches its limits when it strives to describe the final happiness that the human heart longs for. Besides using *heaven* to designate the firmament that is thought of as a hollow sphere above the earth, bearing above it the ocean of heaven, the Bible also uses it to refer to the dwelling place of God (1 Kgs 8:30; Ps 2:4; Mk 11:25; Mt 5:16; Lk 11:13; Rv 21:2), the dwelling place of the angels (Gn 21:17; Lk 2:15; Heb 12:22; Rv 1:4), the dwelling place of Christ (Mk 16:19; Acts 1:9–11; Eph 4:10; Heb 4:14), and the dwelling place of the blessed (Mk 10:21; Phil 3:20; Heb 12:22–24).

As to the salvation and perfection that humans enjoy in this dwelling place, the Bible uses a plethora of expressions to describe it: eternal life, glorification, immortality, incorruptibility, light, peace, harmony with the animals and the cosmos, banquet, wedding feast, homecoming, reign with God, vision of God, union with the Trinity, union with Christ, and communion with the angels and saints.

Heaven is represented as the new paradise, the heavenly temple, the new Jerusalem, the true homeland, the kingdom of God. Clearly, through all these images Scripture is groping after "what eye has not seen, and ear has not heard,/and what has not entered the human heart,/ what God has prepared for those who love him" (1 Cor 2:9; Is 64:3).

In general, as Colleen McDannell and Bernhard Lang have pointed out, images of heaven or paradise in Judeo-Christian theology, pious literature, and art embody two basic ideas: heaven as an intimate union with and contemplation of God (the "theocentric" vision of heaven), and heaven as reunion with spouses, children, relatives, and friends (the "anthropocentric" vision of heaven). These two visions convey the idea that heaven is the fulfillment of the human heart's deepest longings: peace, rest, security, protection, beauty, fellowship with God and with all God's creatures *(Heaven: A History, 353).*

Q. 49. Among the various images of heaven, is there any one that has obtained pride of place in Christian theology?

It seems that in Western theology, the metaphor of seeing God has predominated. The Bible does present the vision of God as the blessed goal of human existence. Matthew 5:8 declares the "clean of heart" blessed because they "will see God." In 1 John 3:2 we are promised that when it is revealed what we shall be, we will be like God, "for we shall see him as he is." But it is Paul's statement that has served as the basis for the view of eternal bliss as vision of God: "At present we see indistinctly, as in a mirror, but then face to face. At present I know partially; then I shall know fully as I am fully known" (1 Cor 13:12).The indistinct vision "in a mirror" and the partial knowledge of God that we now have through faith and the gifts of the Holy Spirit are contrasted with the perfect "face to face" vision and the full knowledge of God in the eschatological age.

The magisterium and theology have developed Paul's notion of face-to-face vision of God to describe our knowledge of God in heaven and refer to it as *"beatific vision."* Pope Benedict XII's constitution *Benedictus Deus* (1336) states: "Since the passion and death of the Lord Jesus Christ, these souls [i.e., the blessed] have seen and see the divine essence with an intuitive vision and even face to face, without the mediation of any creature by way of object of vision; rather the divine essence immediately manifests itself to them, plainly, clearly, and openly *[nude, clare, et aperte],* and in this vision they enjoy the divine essence" *(The Christian Faith, 685).* The *Catechism of the Catholic Church* also uses this visual metaphor to describe eternal happiness (see no. 1028).

Q. 50. With all due respect to the magisterium, I find this talk of heaven as "beatific vision," that is, as seeing "the divine essence" by means of an immediate "intuition," "plainly, clearly, and openly" rather cold and abstract. Could you explain what this "beatific vision" means and how it occurs?

First of all, "vision" is used here analogously to refer not to the physical act of seeing through bodily eyes (God, being spirit, cannot be seen in this way), but to intellectual knowledge. All human knowledge, even the most abstract and universal kind, begins with external sensation and the imagination. For instance, to know what human nature is, one must see, touch, hear, and smell a man or woman before one can form a particular, concrete "image" of this person. From this image one conceives a general, abstract "idea" of the human nature. Of course, what is known is human nature, not the "image" and "idea" of human nature, which are the objective *media* by means of which human nature is known.

If this is true of all our knowledge of the physical world, to which our mind is proportionate, so much more is it true of our knowledge of God, who infinitely exceeds our cognitive capacity. All our knowledge and language about God in this world, either by means of our reason or received through divine revelation in faith, is essentially *analogous*. It arises from our experience with created things and is formulated through images and symbols. To use Paul's expression, we see "indistinctly, as in a mirror." Our knowledge of God begins by *affirming* as true of God the perfections we find in this world (e.g., "God is good"). Then true knowledge of God requires that we *deny* in God all the limitations with which this perfection is realized in this world (e.g., "God is not good the way my father is good"). Finally, knowledge of God demands that we *raise* to the infinite degree the perfection that we attribute to God (e.g., "God is infinitely good").

Alternatively, we may say that there is an analogy or proportionality between the relationship of my father to his finite goodness and the relationship of God to God's infinite goodness. And because ultimately we do not understand what "infinite goodness" means in itself but only the manner in which infinite goodness is not, that is, not finite, we stammer out our knowledge of God in symbols and images and must finally end up in worshipful silence before God.

This knowledge of God, though partial and mediate, is true. Yet, as true as it is, the human mind longs for another, perfect knowledge of God. This is the knowledge of God as God is in God's own self, a kind of direct "intuition," one that is not mediated through created things but given *immediately* and *directly* by God. Since the human mind is finite and incapable of this immediate intuition, its capacity must be enhanced by God's gift of God's own knowledge of self. This grace Christian theology calls the "light of glory." In possessing this "beatific vision," the blessed enjoy eternal bliss.

This notion of beatific vision makes sense within the framework of a realistic theory of knowledge (epistemology), the kind espoused by Thomas Aquinas. No doubt you are right in saying that it is rather cold and abstract in describing what is the fulfillment of the deepest longings of the human heart, for the human heart desires not only an immediate knowlege of God (which is well conveyed by the notion of beatific vision) but also total communion of life and love with the Triune God. In sum, then, the notion of beatific vision, while correct and useful in describing one aspect of eternal happiness, needs to be complemented by other images and concepts provided by the Scriptures.

Q. 51. In which ways can the notion of heaven as beatific vision be complemented by other images?

With the notion of beatific vision as a direct vision of the divine essence and the oft-repeated contrast between faith as an indistinct knowledge and heaven as a face-to-face encounter with God, one runs a great risk of thinking that in heaven we will possess a comprehensive understanding of God and that the mystery of God will be finally dispelled. Of course, this is absolutely false.

To avoid this danger, we need to recover the biblical understanding of God as incomprehensible mystery. God is not a *provisional* mystery or riddle that we are not able to solve now because we lack the necessary intellectual tools but that we will be able to solve in heaven with the aid of the "light of glory." Rather, God is the *absolute* mystery who dwells in inaccessible light. Of course, this unapproachable God has given God's very self to us in revelation and in the incarnation of God's Son, so God, though infinitely distant, has made himself absolutely near to us in grace. Thanks to this divine self-gift to us, we do acquire a certain and sure knowledge of God by means of both our reason and faith. But unlike our knowledge of, for example, a machine, which we can use and control, the knowledge of God is not a penetration into and mastery of God. Rather, like our knowledge of a person we love who always remains a mystery to us, it is a humble and grateful acknowledgment of God's gracious nearness to us precisely *as* incomprehensible mystery and a loving self-surrender to him.

Knowledge of God and recognition of God as incomprehensible mystery are not opposite to each other and do not cancel each other out. On the contrary, they grow in direct proportion to each other: the more one knows God, the more one recognizes God's incomprehensibility, and vice versa. This kind of knowledge of God is ultimately a self-surrender in love to the mystery of God. Thus, the mystery of God is not something that imposes an unfortunate limitation on our beatific vision but is that which makes it possible in the first place.

The beatific vision is not and cannot be the dissolution of the mystery of God. Ultimately, the apparent conflict between the abiding hiddenness of God and the beatific vision can be resolved only if knowledge is raised up into love. Consequently, heaven as beatific vision of the divine essence must be complemented by the notion of heaven as total communion in life and love with the Triune God. In other words, the predominantly visual metaphor for heaven must be enriched by metaphors derived from other senses. Thus, one may say that in heaven, in addition to seeing God face-to-face, we hear God's Word clearly, breathe God's Spirit fully, touch God's life intimately, and taste divine love profoundly.

Furthermore, this notion of heaven as total communion in loving knowledge with the Triune God must be complemented by the notion of heaven as communion with our fellow human beings. Heaven is the "place" where our loving relationships are extended beyond the immediate circle of our family members and friends, whom we will meet again, to include all the human beings who have ever lived. There the "communion of saints" will be realized in its fullness.

Finally, heaven also includes the material universe with all that is present in it, from inorganic things to plants to animals. Though the Bible does not specify what the "new heaven and the new earth" will be made up of, it is not fanciful to imagine that it is no other than *this* universe that Paul describes as groaning, like a woman about to give birth, for redemption and which God will set free from decay to share in the glorious freedom of God's children (Rom 8:20–22).

In sum, heaven is not only vision of the divine essence but also sharing in the life of the Triune God, communion with other human beings, and harmony with the cosmos.

Q. 52. You have just mentioned the Trinity. How are we related to the Triune God in heaven?

To understand how we will be related to the Trinity in heaven, we must understand how we are now related to the Trinity in grace in this life, since grace is a foretaste and anticipation of eternal life. Catholic theological tradition after the Council of Trent (1545–63) used to speak of sanctifying grace primarily as God's supernatural *created* gift infused into the soul and inhering in it, truly transforming it and enabling it to partake in the divine nature. While this view of grace is correct, recently there has been a recovery of a richer doctrine of grace as *uncreated* grace, that is, as nothing other than the Triune God dwelling in the just. The trinitarian nature of heaven is also strongly affirmed by the *Catechism of the Catholic Church* (see no. 1997).

In this participation in the divine life, Christians are not related to God in a *generic* and common way, so that one may say, for instance, that they are children of God, without any difference, whether it is God the Father, God the Son, or God the Spirit. Nor is it enough to say that, while they are related to God in a generic way, this relationship can be *appropriated* to each of the three divine persons in such a way that, though in reality they have the same relation to the three divine persons, this relation is attributed differently to each of them. By virtue of this appropriation one would say, for instance, that we are related to the Father as Omnipotence, to the Son as Truth, and to the Holy Spirit as Love, though we are related to them in an identical way.

On the contrary, it must be said that in grace Christians do not have a generic or an appropriated relationship to the divine essence but a *proper* and truly *differentiated* relationship to each of the three divine persons. By virtue of this kind of relationship, the Christian is the son or daughter of the Father (and not of the Son and the Spirit), the brother or sister of the Son (and not of the Father and the Spirit), and the temple of the Holy Spirit (and not of the Father and the Son). Hence, these relationships are not interchangeable. This is not just an abstract consideration for theologians, but a truth with practical implications for every aspect of Christian life. For instance, if this is true of our relationship to God in grace, we cannot pray to God in the generic sense; rather, we pray to God the Father, the Son, and the Spirit in different ways. As Paul puts it so elegantly, "for through him [Christ] we both have access in one Spirit to the Father" (Eph 2:18).

In light of this, heaven is to be understood not as an indiscriminate intuitive vision of the one "divine essence," but rather as an eternal and perfectly fulfilled relationship of knowledge and love to the Father in the Son by the power of the Spirit; that is, we are given a share in the life of the Trinity itself. Thus, in heaven we relate to God the Father with the same sentiments of love and gratitude as the Son relates eternally to his Father, and we do so by the same power of the Spirit as that with which the Son relates to the Father.

Q. 53. Does the humanity of Christ have anything to do with our happiness in heaven?

Again, the phrase found in Pope Benedict XII's teaching on the beatific vision, that in heaven we see God "without the mediation of any creature by way of object of vision" (see question 49), can be misleading if it is taken to imply that in heaven we can dispense with the mediation of the humanity of Christ. Benedict's insistence on the *immediacy* of the beatific vision of God, without any created intermediary, was meant to highlight the perfection of our heavenly knowledge of God, unimpaired by any distortive and restrictive interposing created reality, and not to disregard the mediation of Jesus. Indeed, rather than being an obstruction to our vision of God, the humanity of Christ was the perfect revelation of God: "No one has ever seen God. The only Son, God, who is at the Father's side, has revealed him" (Jn 1:18). This idea can also be found in John's gospel in Jesus' response to Philip's request that Jesus show him the Father: "Whoever has seen me has seen the Father" (Jn 14:9).

The mediating role that Jesus performed in his earthly existence is not ended with his death, as if the bodily reality that the Logos had assumed in the incarnation were just an instrument that could be discarded once his mission as revealer and mediator was done. On the contrary, Jesus' bodily reality remains the permanent and eternally necessary medium through which the knowledge of God is communicated to us, both now and in heaven, because whatever Jesus has accomplished in his life, including his role as revealer and mediator, was made final, definitive, and permanent in his death and remains so in eternity.

We may therefore say that our "immediate" vision of God in heaven is "mediated" to us through the humanity of Christ. In this way, heaven acquires a Christian form: Christ is the relational space in which our eternal communion with God in knowledge and love is achieved. As the Letter to the Hebrews says, Jesus is continuing his high-priestly ministry in heaven for us, making intercession (Heb 7:25) and offering his once-for-all sacrifice to the Father for us (Heb 9:1–6).

This *christological* structure of heaven is well expressed by Joseph Ratzinger: "Heaven, therefore, must first and foremost be determined christologically. It is not an extra-historical place into which one goes. Heaven's existence depends on the fact that Jesus Christ, as God, is man, and makes space for human exisence in the existence of God himself. One is in heaven when, and to the degree that, one is in Christa....Heaven is thus primarily a personal reality, and one that remains forever shaped by its historical origin in the paschal mystery of death and resurrection" (*Eschatology: Death and Eternal Life,* 234). The *Catechism of the Catholic Church* also strongly emphasizes that heaven is the community of those who are perfectly incorporated into Christ (see no. 1026).

Q. 54. Besides enjoying perfect communion in knowledge and love with the Triune God, what else do the blessed do in heaven now?

United with God the Father in and through Jesus and by the power of the Holy Spirit, the blessed are thereby united also with the "company of angels," the other blessed (some of whom have been declared saints by the church), those who have died and are in the process of purification, and lastly, those who are still living on earth. This fellowship is called the "communion of saints," a phrase that in

Latin *(communio sanctorum)* can mean both "communion of the saints" and "communion in holy things."

The blessed are therefore not cut off from the community of believers who have not yet arrived to eternal happiness. On the contrary, as Vatican II's *Lumen Gentium* affirms, "being more closely united to Christ, those who dwell in heaven fix the whole Church more firmly in holiness, add to the nobility of the worship that the Church offers to God here on earth and in many ways help in a broader building up of the Church (cf. 1 Cor 12:12–27). Once received into their heavenly home and being present to the Lord (cf. 2 Cor 5:8), through him and with him and in him they do not cease to intercede with the Father for us, as they proffer the merits acquired on earth through the one mediator between God and humanity, Christ Jesus" (no. 49). At times, this intercession for and solidarity with us take the form of apparitions and miracles.

Q. 55. In heaven are all the blessed equally blessed, and can they ever lose their blessedness?

Two more points should be made regarding the blessed. First, each will receive the degree of happiness according to his or her merits. The Council of Florence (1439) teaches that the blessed "see clearly God himself, one and three, as he is, though some more perfectly than others, according to the diversity of merits" (*The Christian Faith,* p. 686). This does not mean that some of the blessed are not entirely happy; they are all perfectly and fully happy, but in diverse manners. The differences are not cause for sadness and jealousy but call forth praise of God's glory and wisdom. Secondly, all the blessed are forever united with God and therefore are no longer subject to the possibility of ever losing God. This certainty of being permanently in God's love is one of the reasons for their perfect happiness.

Q. 56. If heaven is such a wonderful communion with the Triune God and the angels and saints, who would choose to go to hell?

Your question underscores the utter absurdity of hell. In essence, hell is the negation of heaven, an existence in alienation from God and the blessed, and hence a contradiction of the deepest longings of the human heart. As Augustine has said in a memorable phrase, God has created us for God, and our heart is restless until it rests in God. Of course, it is not necessary explicitly to choose hell as such to be separated from God and the community of the saints; indeed, rarely does anyone consciously set out to choose hell as an alternative to heaven. On the contrary, we are separated from God ("commit a mortal sin," as moral theologians say) not only when we refuse to love God but also when we refuse to love God's children: "Whoever does not love remains in death. Everyone who hates his brother is a murderer, and you know that no murderer has eternal life remaining in him" (1 Jn 3:14–15). The *Catechism of the Catholic Church* reminds us of Jesus' warning that we shall be separated from him if we fail to meet the needs of the poor and of his brothers and sisters (see no. 1033).

In addition, your question on the absurdity of hell indirectly recalls the point that was made at the beginning of this chapter, namely, that heaven and hell are not two equal options God creates for us and that statements about heaven and hell are not parallel. As I have said, heaven is a reality; hell is a possibility, albeit a very real one, for me first, and perhaps for others.

Q. 57. What does the Old Testament say about the possibility of hell?

Early Hebrew thought includes a belief that all the dead, both good and evil, descended into Sheol, a subterranean place of dust (Jb 17:16), darkness (Jb 10:21), and forgetfulness (Ps 88:12). This Hebrew concept of Sheol is parallel to the Greek idea of Hades, which is conceived of as a place of sadness and gloom (but not punishment) for all the dead.

As the belief in the resurrection began to take shape, the fate of the dead became differentiated: the good are awakened after death to a new, eternal life (Dn 12:2; 2 Mc 7:9, 11, 14, 23) and are received by God (Ps 49:15; Wis 5:15), whereas the wicked are punished (Is 50:11; 66:24; Jdt 16:17; Wis 4:19) and rise to condemnation and shame (Dn 12:2; 2 Mc 7:14). Their punishment is by fire (Is 50:11; 66:24) and worms (Is 66:24), fire symbolizing destruction, and worms, corruption. The apocryphal book of *First Enoch* provides a vivid description of the punishment of persecutors of Israel and Israelite traitors by fire, worms, ice, chains, and darkness.

Q. 58. Did Jesus preach about hell?

In a sense Jesus did not *preach* about hell; his preaching was focused on the kingdom of God and urged his hearers to repent and believe in the good news of salvation. But he also *threatened* those who did not accept his message with divine judgment and the punishment of *Gehenna.* This word is used twelve times in the New Testament to indicate a place of fiery punishment. With the exception of James 3:6, all the texts in the Synoptic Gospels are presented as sayings of Jesus (Mt 5:22, 29, 30; 10:28; 18:9; 23:15, 33; Mk 9:43, 45, 47; Lk 12:5).

The word *Gehenna* is the Greek transliteration of the Aramaic *gehinnam,* which means "Valley of Hinnom" and refers to the valley running south to southwest of Jerusalem. This valley was the scene of the idolatrous worship of the Canaanite gods Molech and Baal. The worship consisted of sacrificing children by passing them through a fire on a high place and into the hands of the gods. Gradually Gehenna came to be called "the accursed valley" or "abyss" and represented the place of punishment of the wicked Jews by fire.

To describe the punishment in Gehenna, Jesus made use of the apocalyptic imagery common in his time: furnace of unquenchable fire, pit, prison, torture chamber, outer darkness, misery, worms that do not die, weeping and gnashing of teeth, destruction of body and soul. In reading these texts it is important to remember what I said about the process of interpreting the Bible, especially in the answers to questions 7 and 8. We need to discover the worlds *behind, in,* and *in front of* these texts on hell, both to understand these texts accurately and to avoid the kind of fundamentalism prevalent in certain circles of Christians.

Q. 59. What are the worlds represented by the biblical texts on hell?

Briefly, the world *behind* these texts is the apocalyptic world, as I have described in chapter 2, especially in the answers to questions 20, 21, and 26. It would be helpful to reread them in conjunction with this answer. It is a world animated by the ardent hope for God's imminent victory over evil powers, for the vindication of God's faithful people, and for the ultimate punishment of God's enemies. Whereas the symbol of the kingdom of God represents the coming salvation by

God, Gehenna stands for the destruction with which Jesus threatened those who were opposed to God. Just as the kingdom of God is presented in various parables, so Gehenna is depicted in different images. Likewise, just as the kingdom parables should not be taken literally, so Gehenna images should not be taken literally either. Indeed, taken at face value, they would cancel each other out. For instance, darkness would be dispelled by fire, and destruction would make corruption redundant.

Thus, rather than investigating the nature of fire, the biological species of undying worms, and the feasibility of gnashing teeth in the beyond, we have to ask what they stand for in terms of the condition of those condemned to exclusion from the reign of God. To understand their meaning, one has to place them in the context of Jewish apocalyptic literature, both canonical (e.g., Daniel) and extra-canonical (e.g., *First Enoch*), the language of which Jesus explicitly used. For example, one could say that fire indicates divine judgment; weeping, the pains or remorse of the damned; gnashing of teeth, their anger; and outer darkness, their despair. It is to be noted that the New Testament language in these descriptions of hell is far more sober and restrained than the fantastic depictions of hell found in the apocryphal books.

Q. 60. What are the worlds *in* and *in front of* these texts on hell?

Jesus' sayings regarding the Gehenna or hell are intended, not to give a description of the place and kinds of punishment of the damned (a sort of "terror in technicolor"), but to serve as a *warning* about the urgency and absolute seriousness of his message regarding the coming reign of God and a *threat* to those who refuse to heed such a message and make an appropriate change of life.

The world *in* these texts, therefore, is not hell as such, about which those texts would give us factual information. Rather, it is constituted by the relationship between Jesus, his person, and his message on the one hand and his hearers, including *us* today, on the other. The people who inhabit that world are not simply those who call their brother a fool (Mt 5:22), those committing sins with their eyes and hands and feet (Mt 5:29, 30; Mk 9:45, 47), those who are afraid only for their bodies and not also for their souls (Mt 10:28; Lk 12:5), those who give scandals, especially to the little ones (Mt 18:9; Mk 9:43), and the scribes and Pharisees (Mt 23:15, 33). We ourselves are the citizens of the world *in* those texts, and Jesus' words about hell are a warning and threat to us as well.

As for the world *in front of* these texts, that is, the way of being that they challenge us to assume, the *Catechism of the Catholic Church* describes it best when it says: "The affirmations of Sacred Scripture and the teachings of the Church on the subject of hell are a *call to the responsibility* incumbent upon humans to make use of their freedom in view of their eternal destiny. They are at the same time an urgent *call to conversion*" (no. 1036). This way of being is nothing other than discipleship of Jesus—to serve God who is both justice and love by serving God's children.

Q. 61. What does the magisterium teach about hell?

The major magisterial documents in which hell is taught are the following: The "Profession of Faith" of Emperor Michael Palaeologus at the Council of Lyon (1274), Pope Benedict XII's constitution *Benedictus Deus* (1336), and the Decree for the Greeks of the Council of Florence (1439). In brief, these documents affirm that there is a hell, that those who die in mortal sin go to hell immediately, and that the punishments of hell are proportionate to their sins.

It is interesting to note that the *Catechism of the Catholic Church* is rather moderate in its statements on hell. It affirms the existence of hell and its eternity (see no. 1035). Rather than speaking of hell as a place, it presents the doctrine of hell in relational terms and explains its possibility in terms of human freedom: "To die in mortal sin without repenting and accepting God's merciful love means remaining separated from God forever by our own free choice. This state of exclusion from communion with God and the blessed is called 'hell'" (no. 1033). Thus, the church's teaching on the reality and eternity of hell amounts basically to saying that it is *possible* that some individuals, by their freedom, can choose to reject God's offer of friendship and love and that this decision will be made definitive and final in dying and death. However, the church does not say whether or not anyone, in fact, has been or will be damned.

As to the pains of hell, theologians used to distinguish between "pain of loss" (i.e., separation from God and deprivation of the beatific vision) and "pain of sense" (physical suffering). The *Catechism of the Catholic Church* quotes biblical imagery of "unquenchable fire" and "furnace of fire" in connection with hell, but with regard to the pains of hell, it simply says, "The chief punishment of hell is eternal separation from God" (no. 1035).

Q. 62. I can understand that somehow we should be punished for our evil deeds, but why should hell be eternal?

The eternity of hell has been, at least since the third century, a stumbling block for believers and unbelievers alike. As we saw in question 38, there is a widespread belief in reincarnation, which is supposed to enable every person finally to achieve liberation. Even if reincarnation were to be rejected, it is still possible to ask whether God, who in infinite mercy and love wills that all human beings be saved (1 Tm 2:3–4), will allow any creatures to suffer separation from God "eternally," without any possibility whatsoever of turning back to God. Will divine omnipotence be vanquished by the finite freedom of God's creatures? What kind of God would "permit" eternal punishment, which seems to be purely vindictive since it will never bring about moral improvement in the person? Even our imperfect system of justice would attempt to correct the criminals rather than merely punish them. Furthermore, will you be perfectly happy in heaven if the one you love most dearly is separated forever from you and suffers the worst possible pains eternally?

These questions and others prompted Origen, a third-century theologian, as well as other church fathers such as Gregory of Nyssa (ca. 330–ca. 395), Gregory of Nazianzus (329–389), and Ambrose (ca. 339–397), to develop a theory of universal salvation or *apocatastasis,* a Greek word meaning restoration. According to this theory, God's grace will ultimately triumph in all intelligent creatures, including the evil spirits, by moving them to accept God's mercy and love.

This theory as proposed by Origen and his followers was condemned by a local synod at Constantinople in 543, and that condemnation was ratified by the fifth ecumenical council held in that city ten years later: "If anyone says or holds that the punishment of the demons and of impious persons is temporary, and that it will have an end at some time, or that there will be a complete restoration *(apocatastasis)* of demons and impious people, *anathema sit*" (John R. Sachs, "Apocatastasis in Patristic Theology," 621).

What this magisterial decision means is that one is not allowed to *affirm* with dogmatic certainty that all *will* be saved and that we must reckon in all seriousness with the *real possibility* that we ourselves may be lost and lost eternally. The ultimate basis for this doctrine is the teaching of the Scriptures and the nature of human freedom, the choices of which are made, as we have seen in the last chapter, irreversible in death.

Q. 63. Still, can we say that the theory of universal salvation makes a lot of sense as something we can and perhaps must hope for?

The key word in your question is *hope*. Though we cannot affirm with certainty that no one will be damned, we may and *must hope* that hell will be finally empty. After all, the church has never affirmed that anyone in fact has been or ever will be damned. As I mentioned in my answer to question 47, among contemporary theologians, Karl Rahner and Hans Urs von Balthasar have developed what they considered an orthodox doctrine of *apocatastasis.*

For Rahner, if we want to develop an acceptable doctrine of universal restoration, we must hold several doctrines, apparently self-contradictory, at the same time. On the one hand, we must maintain the teaching of the Bible that God wants to save all human beings. On the other hand, God's justice must also be affirmed. Furthermore, we must affirm the existence of human freedom, even in relation to God, and therefore every human being must reckon with the possibility that he or she can refuse assent to God. Finally, the freedom and omnipotence of God must be respected; one cannot say a priori what God can or cannot do vis-à-vis human freedom because human freedom is embraced by divine freedom.

How these propositions can be positively reconciled with one another is not immediately clear to us. But to claim the right to deny any one of them on the ground of their presumed mutual irreconcilability is not justified. To affirm outright universal restoration is to jeopardize human freedom, and to deny a priori the possibility of *apocatastasis* is to impose limits on the supreme sovereignty of God's will.

According to Rahner, we know, on a *general* or *theoretical* level, that God wills to save *all* human beings. Whether, in the *concrete,* as applied to *me,* this universal salvific will will in fact be efficacious or not, I cannot say with certainty. I can only hope that it will be so. And since I may and must hope that I will be saved, I may and *must* extend that hope to others, even first to others and only then to myself. So says Rahner: "There is nothing to prevent a Christian's hoping (not knowing) that in practice the final state of every human being, as a result of the exercise of his or her freedom by the power of God's grace, which dwarfs and also redeems all evil, will be such that hell will not exist in the end. Christians may have this hope (first for others and therefore also for themselves) if, within their histories of freedom, they seriously consider the opposite: final damnation" (*Our Christian Faith: Answers for the Future,* 106–7).

Q. 64. Are there other grounds for hoping that all will be saved?

Like Rahner, Hans Urs von Balthasar argues forcefully for the possibility and necessity of a hope for *apocatastasis.* To hope for eternal salvation for oneself and not for all others would be utterly un-Christian, since Christ died for all human beings of all times. It is Christ's solidarity with *all* sinners that requires Christian hope to be universal in scope.

For von Balthasar, the most powerful evidence of Christ's solidarity with all sinners is what he calls the "Mystery of Holy Saturday." He suggests that Holy Saturday does not represent Christ's triumphant entrance to the underworld (Sheol or Hades) but his total solidarity with sinners in death. Christ has completely identified with sinners and their sins. Sinless, he died a sinner, abandoned by God. As God's Son, he experienced the "hell" of his Father's abandonment in a way impossible for any other human person. At the same time, as the one who "descends into hell," he is the symbol of God's unwillingness to abandon sinners, even in the midst of where God, by definition, cannot be.

According to von Balthasar, on Holy Saturday God planted the cross in the heart of hell as a sign of God's unimaginable love and mercy. It is this willingness of God to go to hell itself to be with sinners that, von Balthaar suggests, will melt the resistance of sinners' hardened hearts, not to compel and force human freedom, but to lure and persuade it to accept divine love. This is possible because human freedom is not absolute but, as Rahner has already pointed out, is embraced by the sovereign freedom of God and Christ.

Apocatastasis, then, for von Balthasar as well as for Rahner, is not a positive doctrine that can be affirmed unconditionally but something that all Christians may and must hope for on the basis of the infinite love and power of God as manifested in the cross of Christ. Such a hope, however, cannot be just an idle velleity or a sentimental dream of a bleeding heart. It constitutes a moral imperative—we must act in the hope that all will be saved.

CHAPTER VI
RESURRECTION OF THE DEAD:
A JOYOUS REUNION

Q. 65. We often say that the soul is immortal. What is the difference between "immortality of the soul" and "resurrection of the dead"? Which of the two does the Christian faith teach, the former or the latter?

Some forty years ago, Oscar Cullmann, a Swiss biblical scholar, dramatically highlighted the irreconcilable difference that he claimed exists between the Greek concept of immortality of the soul and the Christian belief in the resurrection of the dead. Immortality of the soul means the survival beyond death of a spiritual element of the human person, called soul, apart from the material element, which is the body. This concept presupposes the Greek dualistic anthropology. The resurrection of the dead is the restoration of life by God to the entire person. According to Cullmann, after death the soul is in a condition of "sleep" from which it will be awakened by God at the resurrection. Cullmann writes: "Belief in the immortality of the soul is not belief in a revolutionary event. Immortality, in fact, is only a *negative* assertion: the soul does *not* die, but simply lives on. Resurrection is a *positive* assertion: the whole man, who has really died, is recalled to life by a new act of creation. Something has happened—a miracle of creation! For something has also happened previously, something fearful: life formed by God has been destroyed" (*Immortality of the Soul or the Resurrection of the Dead?*, 26–27).

If we understand the relationship between the soul and the body to be adversarial, as Plato did (as explained in my answer to question

31), then Cullmann's strictures against the doctrine of the immortality of the soul are well taken. The Bible does not hold that the body *(soma)* is the tomb *(sema)* of the soul from which it is liberated at death. Rather, it views the human person as a unitary being. In the Old Testament, such words as *basar* (flesh), *nephesh* (soul), and *ruah* (spirit) do not refer to three distinct parts that the human person has but three aspects under which the same one person appears: as corporeal; as living; and as sensing, knowing, and willing. All three dimensions are intimately interrelated, so much so that *basar* is said to think, hope, wish, rejoice, be frightened, sin, and so forth, as much as *nephesh* and *ruah*. A term that is functionally related to *nephesh* and *ruah* is *leb* (heart), which is the seat of feeling, thinking, and willing. Furthermore, spiritual functions are ascribed not only to the heart, but also to the bowels, the kidneys, and the liver. It is not until the Greek period, and in the Book of Wisdom in particular (2:22; 3:4), as I have pointed out in my answer to question 29, that we find an approximation to the Greek view of the human person as composed of soul and body and the affirmation of the immortality of the soul.

In the New Testament we also find the trio *soma* (body) or *sarx* (flesh), *psyche* (soul), and *pneuma* (spirit), but again we should not take them to refer to a threefold division in the human person. They should not be understood along the line of the Greek understanding of "body, soul, spirit" as three elements making up the human person. Rather, they should be viewed in continuity with the Old Testament understanding of *basar, nephesh,* and *ruah.* The human person is conceived of as a living totality, an indivisible unity composed of body, soul, and spirit. To express the difference between Greek and Hebrew anthropology in a phrase, we may say that the Greek *has* the *soma,* whereas the Jew *is* the *soma.*

There are, of course, in the New Testament certain passages that may suggest a dualistic conception of the human person. The body appears as a garment or a tabernacle (2 Cor 5:1–10; 2 Pt 1:13; Phil 1:23); the functions of the body are said to be inferior to those of the spirit (1 Pt 2:11; 2 Pt 2:18; 1 Jn 2:16); and marriage seems undesirable (1 Cor 7:1–11). It would be wrong, however, to interpret these texts as though they contradict the overall teaching of the New Testament regarding the fundamental unity of the human person. It is important to note that for the New Testament it is not the body that is evil and leads to evil; rather, evil resides in the "heart." Because of this fundamental unity of the human person, we can use the phrases "resurrection of the *dead*" (as in the Nicene Creed) and "resurrection of the *body*" (as in the Apostles' Creed) as interchangeable. The "body" here refers not simply to the physical reality but to the single entire person as body, soul, and spirit.

Q. 66. Are you suggesting that the doctrine of the immortality of the soul is no longer valid?

Not at all. The *Catechism of the Catholic Church* affirms that every spiritual soul is immortal every spiritual soul is immortal and that it will be reunited with the body at the final resurrection (see no. 366). it will be reunited with the body at the final resurrection (see no. 366). The recent document of the International Theological Commission has also vigorously affirmed the doctrine of the immortality of the soul: "The survival of a conscious soul prior to the resurrection safeguards the continuity and identity of subsistence between the person who lived and the person who will rise, inasmuch as in virtue of such a survival the concrete individual never totally ceases to exist" ("Some Current Theological Questions in Eschatology," 221).

But in interpreting this doctrine one must be careful to avoid four common misconceptions. First, the Christian understanding of the immortality of the soul, as shown above, is quite different from the Platonic doctrine. It presupposes the intrinsic unity of the human person and does not imply a denigration of the body. Second, immortality is not regarded as some "natural" property of the soul; rather, the Bible (Gn 2–3) sees freedom from death as a gift from God who "*alone* has immortality" (1 Tm 6:16) (emphasis added) and as the fruit of the union with Wisdom (Wis 6:18; 8:13, 17; 15:3). Third, death should not be understood as a purely physical event affecting only the "body," with the "soul," being immortal, remaining totally unaffected by it (hence the danger of equivocation in the description of death as separation of the soul from the body, as shown in the reply to question 31). Death is fearsome precisely because it rends asunder the total person in his or her inner core. Fourth, the Christian hope of resurrection is not hope for survival of the soul after death. However one conceives the continuance in existence of the "separated soul," it is a far cry from the biblical belief in the resurrection of the dead as this belief slowly and gradually emerged from the Old Testament and reached fullness in the New Testament.

Q. 67. In answering question 29, you have already explained what the Old Testament holds regarding the resurrection of the dead. What does the New Testament say about it and, more specifically, about the resurrection of Jesus?

It is important to note from the outset that whatever the New Testament has to say about the resurrection of the dead is derived principally from its belief in the resurrection of Jesus. This is the supreme example of how Christ is the model of the afterlife. Consequently, to understand the resurrection of the dead, it is necessary first to state briefly the New Testament faith in the resurrection of Jesus.

As is clear from 1 Corinthians 15:13–14, Jesus' resurrection is the heart of the Christian message, without which our faith is empty and our preaching void. This message, formulated in a series of credal formulas, was received and transmitted by Paul: "For I handed on to you as of first importance what I also received: that Christ died for our sins in accordance with the scriptures; that he was buried; that he was raised on the third day in accordance with the scriptures; that he appeared to Cephas, then to the Twelve. After that, he appeared to more than five hundred brothers at once, most of whom are still living, though some have fallen asleep. After that he appeared to James, then to all the apostles" (1 Cor 15:3–7).

As to the *reality* of the resurrection, it must be said that all attempts at discrediting the resurrection stories by imputing to the apostles either fraud (e.g., they stole the body or invented the story) or credulity or confusion (e.g., they mistook the tomb or were hallucinating) are today judged unsuccessful by most scholars. Indeed, these charges were already taken into account and refuted by the New Testament writers themselves. Acts 10:41 implicitly answers the accusation that the apostles lied; Matthew 27:64 and 28:13 deal with the charge that Jesus' disciples stole his body; and there was repeated insistence on the disciples' initial unwillingness to believe in Jesus' resurrection (Mt 28:17; Lk 24:11, 37; Mk 16:11, 14; Jn 20:25).

This defense of the historicity of Jesus' resurrection does not, however, mean that it is a fact ascertainable by empirical verification (for instance, able to be captured on a camcorder) as would be any other historical fact such as his death on the cross. Indeed, the New Testament does not offer any *description* of Jesus' resurrection as does, for instance, the apocryphal *Gospel of Peter*. Only the *effects* of Jesus' resurrection are narrated, such as his appearances and the changes in his disciples' attitude. Since Jesus' resurrection ushers in the eschatological age, it is both a historical and transcendent event, real indeed but accessible not by means of historical research but only by faith.

In this connection it is important to note that Jesus' resurrection is not a resuscitation, a return to ordinary human existence in the same body. Unlike Lazarus, Jairus' daughter, and the son of the widow of Nain, who were brought back to life and who had to die again, Jesus is portrayed as being raised by God to glory and power and as having conquered death, the "last enemy." Jesus did not come back to life; he was exalted by God and given a name that is above every name so that every tongue will confess that "Jesus Christ is Lord" (Phil 2:11).

Though there are irreconcilable variations in the New Testament accounts of Jesus' resurrection and appearances (Mt 28:1–20; Mk 16:1–20; Lk 24; Jn 20), there is a common conviction that after his death Jesus was raised by God ("resurrection") into glory ("exaltation" and "ascension"). The language and imagery of resurrection, exaltation, and ascension are no doubt drawn from contemporary Jewish apocalyptic, but they are used to convey a real event, a deed that God has done for Jesus, and not simply something that happened to the apostles. The *Catechism of the Catholic Church* strikes a delicate balance between historicity and transcendence when it states: "Although the Resurrection was an historical event that could be verified by the sign of the empty tomb and by the reality of the apostles' encounters with the risen Christ, still it remains at the heart of the mystery of faith as something that transcends and surpasses history" (no. 647).

Q. 68. What about the empty tomb? Isn't it a proof that Jesus was raised?

The evidentiary value of the empty tomb for the resurrection of Jesus is well explained by the *Catechism of the Catholic Church* when it says that the empty tomb is not a direct proof of the resurrection of Jesus but an essential sign of it (see no. 640).

The earliest kerygma as reported by Paul (1 Cor 15:3–7) does not explicitly mention the empty tomb, though it might be implied by the transition between the formula "he was buried" and the formula "he was raised." The absence of the mention of the empty tomb in the earliest preaching does not necessarily mean that the disciples did not know that the tomb was empty or that the tomb itself was not empty; in fact, all four gospels assert that it was. It only meant either that the empty tomb was not then considered an important proof for Jesus' resurrection or that it was not regarded as an essential part of the kerygma. Interestingly, those who were opposed to the affirmation of Jesus' resurrection did not try to disprove the claim that the tomb was empty (something they could have easily done if it were not); rather, they suggested that its emptiness was due to other causes, such as the disciples' stealing Jesus' body.

Q. 69. If the risen Jesus got back his body, why was he not recognized immediately by his followers?

I would like to recall the important fact that resurrection is not reanimation or resuscitation. Jesus did not come back to his former life, reassuming his old body as it had been. In the resurrection Jesus did not simply survive death but vanquished it and was "established as Son of God in power according to the spirit of holiness through resurrection from the dead, Jesus Christ our Lord" (Rom 1:4). His physical body, constituting who Jesus was, shared in his new glorious status. There is therefore identity in difference, continuity in discontinuity; there is the same Jesus but he is in a new mode of existence.

On the one hand, discontinuity and newness account for the fact that the disciples could not recognize Jesus at first: Mary Magdalene thought he was a gardener until he called her name (Jn 20:16); the two disciples on the way to Emmaus mistook him for a stranger until he broke bread with them (Lk 24:31); and the disciples thought he was a ghost until he showed them his hands and his feet (Lk 24:40). Furthermore, Jesus' risen body was not bound by normal physical laws; for example, he could enter the room with locked doors (Jn 20:19).

On the other hand, the New Testament strongly insists that the person who appeared to his disciples after his death was no other than the Jesus whom they had known. Among the four evangelists, Luke and John emphatically affirm the reality of Jesus' (albeit different) body. Luke narrates Jesus' appearance to his disciples, who thought he was a ghost, and has Jesus say: "Look at my hands and my feet, that it is I myself. Touch me and see, because a ghost does not have flesh and bones as you can see I have" (24:39). Luke then reports that Jesus ate a piece of baked fish. John has the "doubting" Thomas put his fingers into Jesus' hands and his hand into Jesus' side to prove the reality of Jesus' body (20:27). In a sense, the empty tomb points toward continuity in discontinuity, identity in difference, between the earthly Jesus and the risen Christ.

Q. 70. How is Jesus' resurrection connected with our own resurrection?

The answer to this most important question can be formulated briefly as follows: Jesus' resurrection is both the *cause* and the *model* of the resurrection of the dead. The principal source for these two ideas is Paul's letters. To understand them rightly, we have to see them in relation to Paul's teaching as a whole, to the communities he was addressing, and to the world of ideas and images to which Paul was indebted.

Let's examine the idea that Jesus' resurrection is the cause of our resurrection first. In the recent past, Jesus' resurrection was seen primarily as a proof and vindication of Jesus' divinity, ministry, and message. While this apologetic view of Jesus' resurrection is not incorrect, it neglects one of the fundamental themes of Paul's "gospel" (Rom 1:16), namely, that Jesus "died for our sins" (1 Cor 15:3) and "was raised for our justification" (Rom 4:25). Again, in 2 Corinthians 5:15 it is said that Christ "died and was raised" for our sake.

Paul develops this idea at great length in his antithesis between the "first man, Adam," and "the last Adam a life-giving spirit" (1 Cor 15:45). In contrasting the consequences of the first Adam's sin with those of the resurrection of the second Adam, Paul affirms unambiguously the causal relationship between Jesus' resurrection and our own: "For since death came through a human being, the resurrection of the dead came also through a human being. For just as in Adam all die, so too in Christ shall all be brought to life" (1 Cor 15:21–22). The expression "in Christ" is to be interpreted in a causal sense: *through* Christ. Christ is the cause of our resurrection. That is why Paul goes on to affirm that Christ is "the firstfruits of those who have fallen asleep" (1 Cor 15:20). Consequently, though all will be brought to life, each one will be raised "in proper order: Christ, the firstfruits; then, at his coming, those who belong to Christ" (1 Cor 15:23). Christ is therefore "the firstborn among many brothers" (Rom 8:29), "the firstborn from the dead" (Col 1:18), "the first to rise from the dead" (Acts 26:23), and "the author of life" (Acts 3:15).

There is another way in which Christ functions as the cause of our resurrection, namely, he gives us his Spirit of life. Indeed, Paul actually says; "the Lord is the Spirit" (2 Cor 3:17). By the power of the Spirit we are made "one body" with Christ (1 Cor 12:12–13), we are "in Christ," and Christ is in us. By this communion with Christ brought about by the Spirit, the "first installment" (2 Cor 1:22; 5:5), we are empowered to overcome death in the future. Through his resurrection, Jesus, "the last Adam," became the "life-giving Spirit" (1 Cor 15:45), that is, one who creates life by imparting to those who have been baptized a share in his Spirit who overcomes death and brings about life.

Q. 71. In which ways is Jesus' resurrection the model for our resurrection?

We could say that Jesus' resurrection is the paradigm of our own resurrection in two ways. First, like Jesus' resurrection, ours will be the work of God. That Jesus' resurrection is God's mighty deed is made clear from what is called "the divine passive." That is to say, out of respect for God's name, instead of using the active voice, "God raised Jesus," the passive voice, "Jesus was raised," is used (e.g., Lk 24:34; 1 Cor 15:4). Of course, to emphasize the divine agency, sometimes the active voice is also used: "God raised him from the dead" (Rom 10:9; 1 Thes 1:10) or "God greatly exalted him" (Phil 2:9). Paul explicitly affirms that just as Jesus' resurrection is a deed of God's creative power, so will be ours: "God raised the Lord and will also raise us by his power" (1 Cor 6:14).

Second, Christ will conform our risen bodies to his own glorious body: "But our citizenship is in heaven, and from it we also await a savior, the Lord Jesus Christ. He will change our lowly body to conform with his glorified body by the power that enables him also to bring all things into subjection to himself" (Phil 3:20–21). Of course, we have to remember that by "lowly body" Paul does not mean only that which is different from the soul, much less a corpse. Rather, he means the entire person with his or her identity, activities, and values; in short, he means the "self" in all its dimensions.

Q. 72. Could you specify in greater detail what the "glorified body" looks like?

Recall what we said above about the risen body of Jesus: in a true sense, it is the same Jesus but in a new mode of existence (question 69). It is the same body, but it is no longer subject to the laws of physics as these are known to us. In his risen body filled with the power of the Spirit, Christ passes from the state of death to another life beyond space and time. But what *kind* of body is a risen body? This is the question that the Corinthian Christians themselves asked. Paul was quite irritated by the question, as is clear from his reply: "You fool! What you sow is not brought to life unless it dies. And what you sow is not the body that is to be but a bare kernel of wheat, perhaps, or of some other kind; but God gives it a body as he chooses, and to each of the seeds its own body" (1 Cor 15:36–38). Perhaps Paul was irritated because the question appeared quite simple and yet he could not answer it clearly.

Indeed, Paul's explication is anything but enlightening. He appeals to two agricultural truisms: a seed will not grow unless it dies, and the plant that grows out of the seed has a different form than that of the seed. He then proceeds to contrast the present body with the glorious body in four sets of characteristics: corruptible versus incorruptible; dishonorable versus glorious; weak versus powerful; and natural versus spiritual (1 Cor 15:42–44).

Using the metaphor of first man/last man, Paul affirms that the present body with its first set of characteristics derives from the "first Adam," who is from the earth, whereas the glorious body with its second set of characteristics is derived from the "last Adam," who is from heaven. So, the risen body is, Paul says, a "spiritual body." This expression, no doubt, sounds like an oxymoron to most people today (and, no doubt, to many Corinthians whom Paul was trying to enlighten), until one realizes that what Paul means is not some kind of improbable hybrid of matter and spirit but a unified, whole human reality ("body") suffused with the power of Christ's life-giving Spirit ("spiritual").

Of course, Paul's explanation is quite unsatisfactory to most of us today because he does not really answer *our* question, which asks about the *empirical* features of the risen body (and those in the business of grading papers know that there is nothing more irritating than answers that do not address the questions or address questions that are not asked!). Paul's answer is *theological,* that is, it tries to show what *God* will do with our human reality when God raises it from the dead.

Q. 73. Still, is it not legitimate to ask, What *type* of body do I rise with?

Of course it is, as long as we are aware that the Bible, not being a book of science, does not provide us with answers to our scientific questions. In general, two issues are involved in the question regarding what type of body we will rise with. The first issue concerns the identity of the risen person, especially its continuity with the person who dies, and the second, the physical characteristics of our risen body. With regard to the identity of the person, recall what was said of the risen Jesus: it is the same yet transformed Jesus. The question here is what constitutes sameness so that we can say that it is the identical person who dies and rises. The answer to this question presupposes answers to a host of other questions such as: What constitutes a human person or "self"? Suppose we say that it is a unity of body and soul, and answer the question of identity by saying, as Thomas Aquinas does, that the selfsameness is effected by "the selfsame soul being reunited to the selfsame body." We may then ask: What constitutes the body? Can we answer by simply pointing to our bones and skin or even to the structure of our DNA and RNA molecules?

In older and simpler days, we could speak, as Thomas did, of "ashes" *(cineres)* and "dust" *(pulveres),* from which the human body will be restored. Unfortunately, such language no longer makes sense to us. Furthermore, even if we could agree on the meaning of body, it still can be asked: What makes it selfsame despite its radical physiological changes throughout life (every seven years, we are told) and total dissolution after death? Can we still hold, as Thomas did, that to achieve bodily selfsameness, not only all the organs of the body will rise again, but also nails and hair (bald folks will be grateful to Thomas for this opinion!) as well as bodily "humors" such as blood and other fluids necessary to bodily integrity (urine, sweat, semen, and milk excepted)?

To make matters a bit more complicated, let's imagine the following scenario (which Augustine [354–430] has mentioned in his book *City of God*. [bk. 22, chap. 20]): A human body is eaten by a fish; that fish is eaten by an animal; that animal is eaten by a person; and, lastly, that person's body is eaten by another person (cannibalism not being unknown). Let's also imagine that this "food chain" goes on billions of times for billions of years (this cannot be ruled out on principle since no one can say when the cosmos will come to an end). The question now is: If we were to understand bodily selfsameness as in Thomas Aquinas' theory (which is assumed on the popular level), how is the risen body of the first human person in the food chain to be reconstituted from his or her "ashes" and "dust" or even from the DNA and RNA molecules?

Q. 74. Do you imply with these questions that there is not and cannot be an identity between the body that dies and the risen body?

Not at all. These questions are intended neither to affirm the impossibility of the resurrection nor to deny the identity between the person that dies and the one that is raised. Rather, they want to show that (1) it is impossible to derive answers to scientific questions regarding the identity between the dead body and the risen body from biblical and magisterial documents; (2) popular notions of personal selfsameness (e.g., possessing the same physical organs) are not helpful to understanding the identity of the risen person; and (3) efforts to say something more specific than the general statement that "one and the same person dies and rises," especially with regard to the risen body, are bound to generate more questions than answers.

Thus, I would argue that texts such as the following cannot be used to defend a particular theory of bodily identity: "We confess the true resurrection of the body of all the dead; nor do we believe that we shall rise in an ethereal body or any other kind of body (as some madly declare), but in that in which we live and exist and move" (Eleventh Council of Toledo in 675). Nor can Leo IX's statement that "I believe also in a true resurrection of this same body which I now bear" be construed to imply that the risen body will have the same physical structure as the body that I now have. The Christian faith only asserts *that* there is an identity in difference, continuity in transformation, between the person that lives and the person that is raised; as to *how* that identity or continuity is preserved, it is a matter for biology, psychology, philosophy, and theology to devise the most reasonable explanation.

My own understanding of the selfsameness of the person is that it does not consist in possessing the same body in the resurrection but in possessing the same history. This history is what I have achieved in my life in and through the many choices I made with my freedom and the deeds through which I carried out those choices. Obviously, because I not only have but also am my body, I cannot become who I am in and through the choices I make and the actions I perform except by means of my body. But though my body changes continously during my life and is dissolved after my death, what remains is my bodiliness, which I have shaped by means of my free choices and actions. It is this bodiliness (which comes to be through my body but is not identical with it) and my "soul" that constitute who I am, and it is this self that is "resurrected." In other words, it is my concrete history, which becomes definitive and final in death, that is "risen," that is, accepted by God and given another existence.

Q. 75. What about the second issue, namely, the physical characteristics of the risen body?

Traditional theology spoke of three sets of characteristics: those belonging to all risen bodies, those belonging only to the bodies of the blessed, and those belonging only to the bodies of the damned. The first set includes immortality (i.e., the risen body is no longer subject to death) and integrity (i.e., endowed with all its members and organs).

The second set of properties belonging to the bodies of the blessed alone include impassibility (excluding all corruption, injury, and pain), splendor (luminous and resplendent), agility (capable of moving with the greatest speed at the command of the soul), and subtlety (capable of penetrating solid objects). The third set of properties belonging only to the bodies of the damned include such deformities and defects as required for the punishment of their sins.

It may be of some interest to note that as to the age of the risen bodies, Thomas Aquinas believes that all will rise at the same age, that is, in their youth, because both childhood and old age would be inappropriate for the risen bodies, the former representing lack of perfection, and the latter moving away from perfection. With regard to height and weight, however, Thomas argues that each will rise according to his or hers that have been acquired in this life, the reason being that there is no ideally perfect weight or height; rather, there are certain degrees of latitude in these respects for each individual (weight watchers, take careful note!).

Of course, with these statements past theologians did not really intend to describe the physical properties of the risen body (after all, they hadn't seen any). Rather, they attempted to articulate what in *their* imagination and culture seems to be the ideal and most perfect body, appropriate for the risen state, just as *ours* have their own set of physical requirements for bodily beauty and perfection. That is why depictions of risen bodies say more about us than about them!

Q. 76. How do we rise? Hasn't Paul described the *manner* of our resurrection?

At first glance, Paul seems to provide us with a scenario of the resurrection of the dead in two important texts. In the first text, he attempted to comfort the Thessalonian Christians for the death of some of their fellow Christians before the coming of the kingdom: "We do not want you to be unaware, brothers, about those who have fallen asleep, so that you may not grieve like the rest, who have no hope. For if we believe that Jesus died and rose, so too will God, through Jesus, bring with him those who have fallen asleep. Indeed, we tell you this, on the word of the Lord, that we who are alive, who are left until the coming of the Lord, will surely not precede those who have fallen asleep. For the Lord himself, with a word of command, with the voice of an archangel and with the trumpet of God, will come down from heaven, and the dead in Christ will rise first. Then we who are alive, who are left, will be caught up together with them in the clouds to meet the Lord in the air. Thus we shall always be with the Lord" (1 Thes 4:13–17).

Leaving aside for the moment consideration of the literary genre of this passage, let us detail the stages of the final resurrection as Paul sees them: (1) descent of Christ from heaven; (2) voice of the archangel; (3) trumpet of the Lord; (4) resurrection of those who have died "in Christ"; (5) lifting up into the clouds ("rapture") of those still alive (among whom Paul counted himself) together with those who have died; and (6) meeting with the Lord in the air. Note that Paul does not say that all the dead will rise but only those who have died "in Christ."

In the second text, found in 1 Corinthians, which explains how Christ, "the firstfruits of those who have fallen asleep" (1 Cor 15:20), will bring about our resurrection, Paul points out the "proper order" in which the final events will take place: "Christ the firstfruits; then, at his coming, those who belong to Christ; then comes the end, when he hands over the kingdom to his God and Father, when he has destroyed every sovereignty and every authority and power" (1 Cor 15:23–24). Further on Paul writes: "This I declare, brothers: flesh and blood cannot inherit the kingdom of God, nor does corruption inherit incorruption. Behold, I tell you a mystery. We shall not all fall asleep, but we will all be changed, in an instant, in the blink of an eye, at the last trumpet. For the trumpet will sound, the dead will be raised incorruptible, and we shall be changed" (1 Cor 15:50–52).

Again, leaving aside the issue of imagery and literary genre, the various events seem to include: (1) the coming of Christ; (2) the sounding of the last trumpet; (3) resurrection of those who belong to Christ; (4) instantaneous transformation of those who are still alive; (5) Christ's victory over all his enemies, in particular death; and (6) Christ the Son's handing of his kingdom over to God the Father and his own subjection to God "so that God may be all in all" (1 Cor 15:28).

Q. 77. What does Paul intend to teach in these two texts regarding the manner of the resurrection of the dead?

The operative word here is *intend,* for more than anywhere else, there is a difference here between what Paul said and what he meant. What he said is couched in characteristically apocalyptic language and imagery: the mystery, the voice of the archangel, the sound of the trumpet, the instantaneous transformation of the dead and the living, rapture, travel into the air, meeting the Lord among the clouds, the contrast between earth and heaven, the separation of this world from the transcendent world, the imminent coming of the final age, and the destruction of every "principality and power."

Obviously, these images cannot and should not be taken literally. Paul is not giving us an anticipatory report of what will transpire at the end of time. He is not satisfying our curiosity about how the resurrection of the dead will occur by providing us with a scenario of the final events. Rather, he is projecting into the end-time, which he thought would come in his lifetime, the event of the resurrection of Jesus, and he is spelling out its effects on those who follow him, dead and living. The world *behind* these texts is the apocalyptic world with its deep conviction about the ultimate vindication of God's faithful ones, here those who have died "in Christ," by means of the bodily resurrection. This world also includes, in the case of the Corinthian community, a group of Christians who deemed themselves to be "spirit-people," filled with "wisdom," mature and perfect, and who looked down upon others whom they regarded as "children" and called "soul-people" and who were, in their view, concerned only with the body and its needs.

The world *in* the text is constituted by God the Father, who raises the dead by the power of the life-giving Spirit; the risen Christ, who is both savior and judge; Christ's own disciples, both dead and living; and the evil powers. In this world, which is his kingdom, Christ rules over all, having destroyed his enemies, including death. He in turn will subject himself to his Father so that "God may be all in all."

The world *in front of* the text is the world of vigilance and hope into which Paul invited the Thessalonians and Corinthians to enter, the world animated and sustained by Christ's promise of return, the world in which the Thessalonians were called to "console one another" with the hope of the resurrection (1 Thes 4:18) and in which the Corinthians were challenged to treat their bodies, including their sexuality, in a manner worthy of the resurrection (1 Cor 5–6).

Q. 78. In spite of your repeated warnings against taking apocalyptic imagery literally and against idle curiosity about the resurrected body, I still feel that if risen persons have "real" bodies, they must do something with them in heaven. First of all, do we rise as male and female?

Before answering this question, I am reminded of some advice given by the Congregation for the Doctrine of the Faith: "When dealing with the human person's situation after death, one must especially be aware of arbitrary imaginative representations: excess of this kind is a major cause of the difficulties that Christian faith often encounters. Respect must, however, be given to the images employed in the Scripture. Their profound meaning must be discerned, while avoiding the risk of overattenuating them, since this often empties of substance the realities designated by the images" ("The Reality of Life After Death," no. 7). There is therefore an extremely delicate hermeneutical task that must be carefully performed lest our eschatological doctrine appear as ludicrous fantasies or empty musings.

With regard to your specific question about whether we will rise in our gender, there are two biblical texts that *seem* to deny the gender differences. First, when the Sadducees, who did not believe in the resurrection of the dead, asked Jesus a trick question about the marital status in the alleged afterlife of the woman who has been married to seven brothers, Jesus replied, "At the resurrection they neither marry nor are given in marriage but are like the angels in heaven" (Mt 22:30). The statement seems to deny any kind of sexual activity in the afterlife. Second, Paul, speaking of the life in Christ after baptism, says, "There is neither Jew nor Greek, there is neither slave nor free person, there is not male and female; for you are all one in Christ Jesus" (Gal 3:28). If there is no longer gender distinction in this life, *a fortiori* there will not be any, it would seem, in the afterlife. Yet, against those who held that because the female gender is imperfect in comparison with the male gender and that because heaven will remove every imperfection women will rise as men, Thomas Aquinas argued that we will rise as male and as female, preserving our gender identity, for the sake of the perfection of the species, which requires sexual diversity. But he hastened to add that there will be no shame for men and women in seeing one another, since there will be no lust to invite them to shameful deeds that are the cause of shame.

As to the words of Jesus to the Sadducees, it may be argued that these do not deny gender differences but only sexual activities in the afterlife. Similarly, Paul's affirmation is intended not to wipe out gender identity but to disallow it as the basis for lessening the unity of Christians with Christ and with one another.

Q. 79. Do you mean that there will be no sex in heaven even if we have real male and female bodies?

This is, not surprisingly, one of the most frequent questions asked about the afterlife. In his idiosyncratic book entitled *Everything You Ever Wanted to Know About Heaven...But Never Dreamed of Asking,* Peter Kreeft raises fourteen questions about heaven. In spite of his advice to practice the Socratic wisdom of "learned ignorance" (pp. 117–32), he gives, with unflinching intrepidity, resolute answers to questions such as whether we will wear clothes in heaven (yes, we will, he assures us, and our heavenly clothes may express our earthly story and success, so that "Socrates will have his philosopher's robe"!) and whether there are animals, especially pets, in heaven (why not, he expostulates, since God, who raises up grass, can certainly raise dead cats!).

Besides these questions that a few intrepid souls may dream to ask, Kreeft also raises your question, Is there sex in heaven? and devotes one entire chapter to the answer (pp. 117–32)! After some philosophical ruminations on sex, he comes to answer the question by reflecting on the purpose of bodily sex organs. Will there be sexual intercourse in heaven? Not for "baby-making" and not for "marriage," he declares, but "certainly for spiritual intercourse" (p. 129). By that he means "something more specific than universal charity," a "special communion with the sexually complementary; something a man can have only with a woman and a woman only with a man" (p. 129).

Of course, since who we are, even in the risen life, necessarily includes our bodiliness, as I have argued above, we cannot but preserve our sexuality in the afterlife. In this sense, we will relate to each other as men and women, and not as some genderless beings. But whether we will engage in actual sexual intercourse, I would rather profess "learned ignorance."

Q. 80. But, surely, even in this life sexual intercourse is not only for "baby-making," to use Dr. Kreeft's expression, for which there seems to be no longer any need in heaven. Isn't sexual intercourse also an expression of love?

While there have been theologians (e.g., Thomas Aquinas) who deny the continuation of nutrition, sexual intercourse, and generation in heaven on the ground that there is no longer the need to replenish the body and to multiply the human species, there are others who think that sexual intercourse for love's sake will continue. For instance, Milton (1608–74) introduced in *Paradise Lost* the idea that sexual intercourse between Adam and Eve made up an essential ingredient in the perfect society prevailing before the Fall. And though he did not speculate on the existence of conjugal love in eternal life, he did affirm that the angels in heaven experience a kind of love not unlike that of Adam and Eve. William Blake in his paintings and engravings *"The Last Judgment," "Vision of the Last Judgment," "The Meeting of a Family in Heaven," "The Day of Judgment,"* and *"Epitome of Hervey's 'Meditation among the Tombs'"* shows couples in loving embraces in heaven. More explicitly, Charles Kingsley (1819–75), the chaplain to Queen Victoria, argued that in heaven it is not marriage but *marrying* that does not exist, and therefore sexual enjoyment will not cease.

Whatever the case may be, it must be said that these affirmations by poets and artists should not be taken as *factual statements* about what risen persons will do with their bodies but rather as *expressions of the hope* that whatever brings happiness and communion on earth will find its most perfect fulfillment in heaven. At any rate, with regard to this question as well as to others that demand factual knowledge of the afterlife, a humble silence or at least a modest reticence is appropriate, acknowledging a proper "learned ignorance" and avoiding the all-too-common danger of fashioning a heaven to fit our own wishes and desires, turning it into a romantic Victorian cottage, a fun-filled vacation resort, or a tranquil retirement village.

Q. 81. At the resurrection, do we meet other people, especially our family and friends, so that we can say that it is a joyous reunion?

Certainly one of the most enduring visions of heaven is that of a place where we meet again those who have been separated from us by death. As we have seen, people with near-death experiences almost invariably recount meeting with their loved ones. The resurrection of the dead not only concerns the reunion of my soul with my body but also the social reunion of myself and the other members of the Body of Christ, particularly my family and my friends. This belief is expressed in "in memoriam" sections of newspapers announcing the death of the deceased or offering condolences, and it is engraved on grave markers with simple epitaphs such as "till we meet again." This hope for reunion is also expressed by the church at the moment of final farewell, shortly before burial:

> Our prayers are now ended, and we bid our last farewell. There is sadness in the parting, but it should fill us with new hope, for one day we shall see our brother (sister) again and enjoy his (her) love. By God's mercy, we who leave this church today in sorrow will be reunited in the joy of God's kingdom. Let us comfort one another in the faith of Jesus Christ. (The Rites of the Catholic Church, 706)

It will be a joyous reunion not simply because we see again people we love and/or who love us after a painful separation; not only because we are now brought to perfection in our entire reality as body and soul; not only because now the Body of Christ has achieved its full stature; but also because, I surmise, we *may* find people who we thought have been lost and excluded from communion with God and us, people we have condemned because of their evil deeds, and people whom we have doomed to hopelessness yet, by the miracle of God's amazing grace, have been brought into the community of the saints.

Q. 82. All this talk about the resurrection at the end of time makes it so abstract and remote. Is there any way in which even now we can experience the new life of the resurrection?

Of all the sacraments, the Eucharist is the most powerful symbol of the future resurrection. It is a sure pledge of eternal life, an antidote against eternal death, and a food that makes us live forever with Jesus Christ (see the *Catechism of the Catholic Church,* no. 1405).

The causal link between the Eucharist and the resurrection is made explicit in John 6:54: "Whoever eats my flesh and drinks my blood has eternal life, and I will raise him on the last day." Even the transformation of bread and wine into the body and blood of Christ is a symbol of the transformation of our mortal bodies into immortal, risen bodies. Furthermore, the fact that the Eucharist is celebrated on Sunday, "the day of the resurrection," intimates the intrinsic connection between the Eucharist and the resurrection. It is with reason, then, that the Eucharist is called the "medicine of immortality." By participating in the Eucharist, and especially by communicating with Christ's body in the bread and wine, we receive a taste of the future resurrection. As Geoffrey Wainwright writes, "What is true of the inanimate creatures of bread and wine cannot be less true of the body of the man who consumes them at the eucharist, and so we may be confident that the human body shares, and will continue to share, in an appropriate way in that personal obedience to a loving King in which the highest and ultimate destiny of man consists" (*Eucharist and Eschatology,* 149).

CHAPTER VII
THE FULFILLMENT OF HOPE:
BACK TO THE EARTH

Q. 83. Together with the resurrection of the dead, we profess in the Creed that Jesus will "come again to judge the living and the dead." What does Paul say about the "coming again" of Jesus?

This "coming again" of Jesus is often referred to with the Greek word *parousia.* In classical Greek, the word usually means "arrival" or "presence"; in Hellenistic Greek, it can mean the official visit by a king. In the New Testament, *parousia* is used to indicate Christ's expected appearance in glory at the end of time. It is not used to refer to Christ's first coming on earth, presumably because he came then in humility and not in glory. The common expression "second coming" is not found in the New Testament (though we read in Hebrews 9:28: "Christ…will appear a second time"). At times the word *epiphaneia,* meaning manifestation, is used instead of *parousia* (2 Thes 2:8; 1 Tm 6:14; 2 Tm 4:1, 8; Tit 2:13). Lastly, *apocalypsis,* meaning uncovering, is also used sometimes in the same sense as *parousia* (1 Cor 1:7; 2 Thes 1:7; 1 Pt 1:7; 4:13).

Of course, the notion of the coming of God is deeply rooted in the Hebrews' experience of God's multiple presences in the course of their history, especially with the prophets' announcement of the "day of Yahweh," a day of both salvation and judgment. In apocalyptic literature, as we have seen, the expectation of the coming of God as the vindication of the righteous was greatly intensified.

In the New Testament, this expectation is proclaimed to have been fulfilled in the life and ministry of Jesus; in his person the end-time, signified by the coming of the kingdom of God, has been inaugurated. After his death and resurrection, there grew among his immediate followers, on the basis of Jesus' own promise, an intense expectation that he would soon come back in glory as Lord and Judge.

The earliest expression of this faith in the parousia of Christ is found in the two Pauline texts that we have already examined in questions 75–76, namely, 1 Thessalonians 4:13–17 and 1 Corinthians 15:23–28; 50–52; hence, we will pass over them here. There is, however, another important text that we must now consider, namely, 2 Thessalonians 2:1–12.

Contemporary biblical scholarship tends to regard 2 Thessalonians as a pseudoepigraph, that is, as a work written by someone other than Paul who, in Paul's name, penned this letter to the Thessalonian community to dispel one of the misunderstandings of Paul's teaching about the "day of the Lord." In his letter to the Thessalonians, Paul had assured them that the day of the Lord would be coming soon. As time passed, perhaps a decade or more after Paul's death, the Thessalonian Christians began wondering whether Paul's preaching about Christ's imminent return in glory was correct. The writer of 2 Thessalonians attempted to deal with this faith crisis, first, by reaffirming the belief in Christ's parousia and, second, by interpreting it in the new context.

In vivid language drawn from the Old Testament apocalyptic, the writer announced that those who troubled the Thessalonians would be punished "at the revelation of the Lord Jesus from heaven with his mighty angels, in blazing fire." These will "pay the penalty of eternal ruin, separated from the presence of the Lord and from the glory of his power, when he comes to be glorified among his holy ones and to be marveled at on that day among all who have believed" (2 Thes 1:7–10).

While strongly affirming the parousia, the writer chided those Thessalonians who had been alarming the community with their statement (with the alleged support of one of Paul's letters!) that the day of the Lord was at hand (2:2). In an attempt to reinterpret Paul's eschatological teaching to meet the challenges of the community, the author claims, in veiled language, that certain "signs," not yet forthcoming, must precede Christ's parousia. It would not be at hand "unless the apostasy comes first and the lawless one is revealed, the one doomed to perdition, who opposes and exalts himself above every so-called god and object of worship, so as to seat himself in the temple of God, claiming that he is a god"

(2:3–4). Again, the imagery is drawn from Old Testament apocalyptic literature, especially Daniel. The "lawless one," "the one doomed to perdition," who attempts "to seat himself in the temple of God" may refer to Antiochus IV Epiphanes (Dn 12:11) or possibly to the Roman emperor Caligula (Mk 13:4).

The author goes on to allude obscurely to both something (a force) and someone (a person) currently "restraining" the "lawless one" for a time. After this restraining power or person is removed, "then the lawless one will be revealed, whom the Lord [Jesus] will kill with the breath of his mouth and render powerless by the manifestation of his coming *[parousia],* the one whose coming springs from the power of Satan in every mighty deed and in signs and wonders that lie" (2:8–9). The restraining force and person have been variously identified as the Roman Empire, the Roman emperor, some cosmic or angelic power, Michael the archangel, the preaching of the gospel, and Paul himself. Once again, the language is apocalyptic, suggesting a "holy war" between the forces of evil and Christ.

It is interesting to note that the author, while strongly insisting on the reality of Christ's parousia, carefully avoids any speculation on the precise moment of its arrival in terms of clock-and-calendar time and eschews any description of the end-time scenario. His only interest is to restore to the community the faith in the ultimate victory of Christ over all evils. Indeed, such is Christ's power!

Q. 84. Besides Paul, do other New Testament writers speak about the parousia?

In my answers to questions 23–25 I have alluded to the teaching of the Synoptic Gospels, John, and Revelation about the parousia of Christ as judge of the living and the dead. Indeed, Christ's second coming in glory is presupposed in all the eschatological discourses, also known as the Olivet Discourse, because they allegedly took place on the Mount of Olives (Mt 24; Mk 13; Lk 21). There is also ample evidence for the belief in the imminent coming of Jesus in chapters 1, 19, and 22 of Revelation.

The teaching of the New Testament on the parousia can be briefly summarized as follows: (1) It will occur "at the end of time"; in this sense it is different from other "comings" of Jesus, such as his coming in the flesh, in grace, in the Eucharist, and at our death. (2) Jesus himself will come in person, not his representative, whoever that person may be, angelic or human: "They will see the Son of Man coming upon the clouds of heaven" (Mt 24:30). (3) Jesus' coming will be preceded by signs of various kinds. (4) His coming is therefore recognizable and public. (5) His coming is powerful and glorious; he is, in the words of Revelation, the rider on the white horse, the King of kings and Lord of lords (chap. 19). (6) Though preceded by signs, the parousia will be sudden and unexpected: "The day of the Lord will come like a thief at night" (1 Thes 5:2), even if we are not entirely in the dark about it (1 Thes 5:4).

In John, the coming of the Spirit-Paraclete is presented as a compensation for the return of Jesus; indeed, the coming of the Paraclete and the return of Jesus are closely linked (Jn 14–17). The Paraclete's function is to act as the memory of Jesus to remind the disciples of what Jesus has said and to teach them everything (Jn 14:26). Though there is reference to Jesus' "coming back" to take his disciples with him so that where he is they may also be (Jn 14:3; see also 21:21–23), the main focus of the Johannine gospel is on Jesus' "first coming" in the flesh, to which both the community and the Paraclete-Spirit bear witness.

Q. 85. But obviously Jesus has not come in glory as was expected by Paul and other early Christians. Wasn't the parousia delayed?

There is little doubt that Paul and other early Christians thought that Christ would return in glory within their lifetimes, even though they did not fix a specific date for the parousia. Nor is there any doubt that the parousia did not materialize *in the manner they expected.* Furthermore, that the delay of the parousia caused problems for the early Christians is borne out by the disturbances in the Thessalonian community mentioned in question 83.

There is even an explicit reference to the "scoffers" who mocked the delay of the parousia: "Where is the promise of his coming? From the time when our ancestors fell asleep, everything has remained as it was from the beginning of creation" (2 Pt 3:4–5). The scoffers of the parousia based their scoffing on two grounds: (1) There has been no judgment by God in past history; (2) God does not act in creation. The author of 2 Peter rebuts the scoffers in three ways: (1) God did judge the world, by water at the time of Noah and by fire at Sodom and Gomorrah (3:5–7). (2) God's time is mysterious and incalculable: "With the Lord one day is like a thousand years and a thousand years like one day," so that one cannot speak of delay (3:8). (3) If there has been a delay, God's patience allowed it for our own good, so that we might have sufficient time for repentance (3:9).

There might be a similar questioning about the delay of the parousia in the epilogue of the Gospel of John. John 21:23 indicates that there was an expectation among the members of the community of the Beloved Disciple that he would not die before the return of Jesus. Now that he has, a question mark has been placed about the future coming of Jesus.

Q. 86. How did the early Christians deal with this delay?

Early Christianity had ample resources to deal with the ambiguity of the nonfulfillment of the parousia. First of all, as we have seen in the answer to question 83, the author of 2 Thessalonians, though reaffirming the belief in the parousia, refrained from offering precise information on the time and place of this event. With the help of apocalyptic stock-in-trade, he alluded to some holy war in which the "lawless one" will be killed by Christ at his coming. What he was interested in was to keep the faith in the parousia without taking up the losing game of predicting its date and time. In other words, he was able to maintain a lively sense of the *kairos,* the moment of salvation, without falling into the *chronos,* the clock-and-calendar time.

Second, the author of 2 Thessalonians shifted the community's attention away from idle and fruitless crystal ball gazing and urged it to undertake activities for the welfare of its members. More specifically, he warned that "if anyone was unwilling to work, neither should that one eat" (3:10). In this way, he was able to show that faith in the afterlife should not detract from one's commitments to the present world.

Third, as Luke has done in his twin works, it is possible to transform the period between Christ's ascension and his return into a time of the church, the "intermediary age," in which expectation of the parousia is not an empty waiting but a force driving the church's evangelization.

In this way, the present life of the church becomes a glimpse, a foretaste, of the kingdom of God, just as the Spirit empowers Christians even in this world to participate in "the powers of the age to come" (Heb 6:5).

Q. 87. What are the signs by which we can discern the second coming of Christ?

Interestingly enough, this same question was asked Jesus by the disciples themselves: "Tell us, when will this happen, and what sign will there be of your coming, and of the end of the age?" (Mt 24:3). Before discussing the "signs of the times," it is useful to remember that the Olivet Discourse concerns both the destruction of Jerusalem (which occurred in 70 C.E.) and the eschatological second coming at "the end of the age." This dual focus makes the interpretation of the signs of the end-time a very risky enterprise. It is also necessary to remember that biblical prophecies very often *foreshorten* the time period in which events are said to occur and *foreshadow* the eschatological events in the events of history. In other words, biblical prophecies do not spell out the possibly long intervals that separate different foretold events (e.g., the destruction of Jerusalem and the end of time) and therefore give the impression that these events are contemporaneous happenings (foreshortening). Biblical prophecies also see historical events as partial fulfillment of future eschatological events (e.g., the destruction of Jerusalem as foreshadowing the end of the age).

With these caveats in mind, let us now list some of the signs of the times. (1) False messiahs: "For many will come in my name, saying, 'I am the Messiah,' and they will deceive many" (Mt 24:5). (2) Worldwide conflicts: "You will hear of wars and reports of wars....Nation will rise against nation, and kingdom against kingdom" (Mt 24:6–7). (3) Natural disasters: "There will be famines and earthquakes from place to place" (Mt 24:7). (4) Persecution of believers: "They will hand you over to persecution, and they will kill you. You will be hated by all nations because of my name" (Mt 24:9). (5) Increase in evil: "Because of the increase of evildoing, the love of many will grow cold" (Mt 24:12). (6) Worldwide preaching of the gospel: "And this gospel of the kingdom will be preached throughout the world as a witness to all nations" (Mt 24:14). (7)

The "desolating abomination": "When you see the desolating abomination spoken of through Daniel the prophet standing in the holy place (let the reader understand), then those in Judea must flee to the mountains." (Mt 24:15). The desolating abomination refers to the events of 70 C.E. in which the Roman legions desecrated the Temple by carrying in their banners and insignia, tore down the Temple, burnt it, and carried its treasures back to Rome. (8) Then comes the "great tribulation, such as has not been since the beginning of the world until now, nor ever will be" (Mt 24:21). (9) Finally, "immediately after the tribulation of those days,/the sun will be darkened,/and the moon will not give its light,/and the stars will fall from the sky,/and the powers of the heavens will be shaken./And then the sign of the Son of Man will appear in heaven, and all the tribes of the earth will mourn, and they will see the Son of Man coming upon the clouds of heaven with power and great glory. And he will send out his angels with a trumpet blast, and they will gather his elect from the four winds, from one end of the heavens to the other" (Mt 24:29–31).

What are we to make of these signs? Clearly, they are a grab bag of apocalyptic imagery that cannot and should not be taken literally as a blow-by-blow description of the end-time scenario. On the other hand, there is a reference to a historical event (the "desolating abomination") that serves as a foreshadowing of the events of the end-time. As mentioned above, the Olivet Discourse has a double focus. On the one hand, as far as the destruction of the Temple is concerned, Jesus' prediction proved to be true. Perhaps that is what Jesus meant when he said, as reported in Matthew 24:34: "Amen, I say to you, this generation [i.e., his hearers] will not pass away until all these things [i.e., the destruction of Jerusalem] have taken place [i.e., some forty years later]." On the other hand, as far as the eschatological events are concerned, Jesus contented himself with giving apocalyptic stock-in-trade signs and urged his audience to be vigilant: "Therefore, stay awake! For you do not know on which day your Lord will come" (Mt 24:42).

Q. 88. But surely someone could rely on these signs to predict the day of the second coming of Jesus? Has anyone tried to do this?

In spite of Jesus' explicit statement, "But of that day and hour no one knows, neither the angels of heaven, nor the Son, but the Father alone" (Mt 24:36), there has been no lack of self-styled prophets, in olden days as well as in our times, who claim to have received secret revelations from God regarding the time and place of the parousia. As early as the middle of the second century, Montanus, with two women associates, Prisca and Maximilla, claimed that the heavenly Jerusalem would soon descend in Pepuza, a small village in Phrygia. In the early Middle Ages some people thought that Christ would come back about 1000 C.E.; their reasoning was that since one day with God is like a thousand years (2 Pt 3:8) and since the creation took place in 4000 B.C.E., Christ would return at the beginning of the earth's sixth millennium, that is, 1000 C.E. In the nineteenth century, a Roman Catholic priest predicted that 1848 would be the year of the parousia. The Englishman Michael Baxter, unfazed by his repeated errors, made numerous predictions about the second coming between 1861 and 1908. At one point he predicted that Jesus would come back on March 12, 1903, between 2:30 and 3:00 in the afternoon!

In this country, William Miller, the forerunner of the Seventh-Day Adventists, settled on 1843 as the date for the parousia. Charles Taze Russell, the founder of the Jehovah's Witnesses, was much given to date setting, choosing 1874 and then 1914 as the pivotal years. Recently, a group of Koreans selected 1994 as the time of the end of the world. As the millennium is drawing to a close, it is to be expected that eschatological fervor will be rekindled and more people will be tempted to take up again the risky business of predicting the day of the parousia.

As is clear from the fact you are reading my present book on eschatology, all these predictions about the end-time have been proved false. In this matter, it is wise to heed Thomas Aquinas' observation concerning predictions of the end-time. Referring to Matthew 24:36, he says: "For what Jesus refused to tell the apostles, he will not reveal to others. Therefore, all those who have been misled to reckon the aforesaid time have so far proved to be untruthful....The falseness of these calculations is evident, as will likewise be the falseness of those who even now cease not to calculate" (*Supplement to Summa Theologiae,* q. 77, a. 2). Of course, given human curiosity and credulity, repeated failures in the past will not deter others from trying again, as Thomas shrewdly observed, and, like inveterate gamblers, they think they will get it right this time.

Q. 89. In the New Testament there is mention of the "antichrist" appearing at the end of time. Who is the antichrist, and what does he or she do?

The expression *antichristos* is found only in the Johannine letters (1 Jn 2:18, 22; 4:3; 2 Jn 7). The *anti* probably indicates opposing Christ rather than merely claiming falsely to be the Christ. If this is true, then the idea behind the antichrist is widespread in the Bible. For instance, we should see the antichrist in such Old Testament passages as Daniel 7:7 f., 21 f.; and in 2 Thessalonians 2 and Revelation, which speak of the strong opposition of the forces of evil against Christ in the last days.

Paul does not use the word *antichrist* but writes about the "lawless one," "the one doomed to perdition" who "opposes and exalts himself above every so-called god and object of worship, so as to seat himself in the temple of God, claiming that he is a god" (2 Thes 2:3–4). He is not Satan but acts as his instrument to challenge the rule of Christ. Christ, of course, will triumph in this cosmic battle, killing his opponent with the simple "breath of his mouth" (2 Thes 2:8). In the meantime, this "lawless one," though already at work, is being restrained by a person and/or a force that, as I said in my answer to question 83, has been variously identified as the Roman Empire, the Roman emperor, some angelic power, the preaching of the gospel, or Paul himself.

The concept of the antichrist is presumed to be familiar to the Johannine community. He is supposed to come at the end-time: "Children, it is the last hour; and just as you heard that the antichrist was coming, so now many antichrists have appeared" (1 Jn 2:18). Indeed, there is more than one antichrist (1 Jn 2:18). The defining feature of the antichrist is denial of the Father and the Son (1 Jn 2:22). This denial is explained more specifically as denial of "Jesus Christ as coming in the flesh" (2 Jn 7), which is tantamount to rejecting the very foundation of the Christian faith. The antichrist is therefore the sum total of all opposition to Christ.

The Book of Revelation portrays two beasts, one that came up from the sea and another that came out of the earth. The first appears like a leopard with the feet of a bear, the mouth like a lion, ten horns crowned with diadems, and seven heads inscribed with blasphemous names (Rv 13). It has the strength of the dragon, who is the devil, and possesses its throne, makes people adore it, blasphemes God, and persecutes Christians. Its name, which is not given, corresponds to the number 666. In

19:19 f. it joins battle with Christ but is vanquished and cast into the sea of fire.

The beast that came out of the earth resembles a lamb and has two horns but talks like the dragon. It performs wonders and leads people astray, causing them to worship the first beast or its image. Whoever refuses to do this is slain. It is the "false prophet" (Rv 16:13; 19:20; 20:10) who, together with the other beast, is cast into the sea of fire (Rv 19:20).

Q. 90. Can you say more definitely who the antichrist is in history? Was Hitler the antichrist?

As is clear from my answer above, it is easier to say what the antichrist does than *who* he or she is. Again, the language is quintessentially apocalyptic. On the one hand, it is possible to see in the antichrist a personification or a collection of all the forces of evil fighting against Christ and his followers. On the other hand, he has been identified with certain historical figures. Given the statement that his name is said to equal 666 (each of the letters of the alphabet in Hebrew as well as in Greek has a numerical value), various candidates have been named to provide that infamous number. The most likely is the Roman emperor Caesar Nero, whose name, when written in Hebrew characters, has the numerical value of 666. The antichrist was also identified with various popes or the papacy itself by the Protestant reformers. More recently, Hitler and various Communist leaders were chosen to fill the position. Even Saddam Hussein was demonized as the antichrist.

Perhaps it would not be amiss to point out that the tendency to see the antichrist in others, to demonize our enemies and those who disagree with us, is indeed one of the hallmarks of the antichrist. Recall that according to the First Letter of John, the antichrist is the one who denies the incarnation of the Son in the flesh. We can deny the truth of the incarnation not only intellectually but also (and very often) by not recognizing Jesus "incarnated" in his brothers and sisters. Surely, calling someone the antichrist or the "evil empire" because he or she does not agree with our politics and theology can be counted as not recognizing Christ incarnated in his members.

Q. 91. Recently, in conversations about the end of the millennium, I have heard people, especially Protestants, say that we are now in the last "dispensation." What does this mean?

The term is derived from the Latin *dispenso,* "to weigh out" or "to administer as a steward." In theological parlance, it is used to designate the system some think God has established to regulate humanity's obedience to God in the course of history. There have been numerous attempts at outlining the various dispensations of God's plan. Dispensationalists trace their origins to the teaching of John Nelson Darby of Dublin (1800–82), one of the early leaders of the Plymouth Brethren.

The most popular form of the system is found in the Scofield Reference Bible (1902–9; revised 1917, 1966). According to this view, although the history of salvation is one, God has divided it into seven dispensations or stages, in each of which people have been given a specific test by God. The seven dispensations are: (1) from innocence (Gn 1:28) to the expulsion from Eden; (2) from conscience or moral responsibility (Gn 3:7) to the Flood; (3) from human government, in which God delegated areas of divine authority to human beings (Gn 8:15), to the call of Abraham; (4) from the promise, the test of Israel's stewardship of divine truth (Gn 12:1), to the giving of the Law on Sinai; (5) from the giving of the Law and disciplinary correction (Ex 19:1) to the death of Christ; (6) from the church, the dispensation of the Spirit (Acts 2:1), to Christ's return; and (7) from the kingdom of God for a thousand years (Rv 20:4) to the eternal state.

Obviously, the last two dispensations are of great relevance to the issue of eschatology. In particular, we are now in the sixth dispensation, waiting for Christ's return, and the coming end of the millennium makes dispensationalists wonder whether the end of the world, together with Christ's rule for a thousand years, is also approaching.

Q. 92. In this dispensationalist scheme, why is the sixth dispensation of particular importance?

It is believed that at the end of this dispensation Christ will return and that then the "rapture" will occur. In 1 Corinthians 15:51–52, Paul states that when Christ returns to raise the dead, believers who are still alive will be "changed" in an instant. In 1 Thessalonians 4:17, he adds that they will be "caught up" (rapture), together with those who have died, to meet the Lord in the air. Jerry Falwell, a fundamentalist preacher, imagines the rapture this way: "You'll be riding along in an automobile; when the trumpet sounds, you and the other born-again believers in that automobile will be instantly caught away—you will disappear, leaving behind only your clothes....That unsaved person or persons in the automobile will suddenly be startled to find the car moving along without a driver, and the car suddenly somewhere crashes" (quoted in J. Anthony Lukas, "The Rapture and the Bomb," *New York Times Book Review,* 8 June 1986, 7).

Some dispensationalists distinguish between a first and secret return of the Lord for the rapture and his final public return in glory after a seven-year period of tribulation upon earth (Rv 6:19) to establish his millennial kingdom. In this scenario, which is widely accepted by evangelical and fundamentalist Christians, there are the following successive events: (1) the rapture (1 Thes 4:15–18); (2) a seven-year tribulation (Rv 6:12–17); (3) Christ's second coming (Mt 24:30); (4) Christ's thousand-year messianic reign (Rv 20); (5) the destruction of the present world (2 Pt 3:10); (6) the last judgment (Mt 25:31–46); and (7) the coming of the new heaven and the new earth and eternity (Rv 21–22).

Q. 93. In the scenario of the end-time proposed by the evangelicals, there is mentioned a thousand-year messianic reign. What is the biblical basis for this belief?

The notion that Christ will reign for a thousand years is based on a vision related in Revelation 20:1–10:

> Then I saw an angel come down from heaven, holding in his hand the key to the abyss and a heavy chain. He seized the dragon, the ancient serpent, which is the Devil or Satan, and tied it up for a thousand years and threw it into the abyss, which he locked over it and sealed, so that it could no longer lead the nations astray until the thousand years are completed. After this, it is to be released for a short time.
>
> Then I saw thrones; those who sat on them were entrusted with judgment. I also saw the souls of those who

had been beheaded for their witness to Jesus and for the
word of God....They came to life and they reigned with
Christ for a thousand years....

When the thousand years are completed, Satan will
be released from his prison. He will go out to deceive the
nations....The Devil who had led them astray was thrown
into the pool of fire and sulfur, where the beast and the false
prophet were.

Ever since this vision was written down, countless interpretations
have been given to it. The belief that Christ and his followers will reign
for a thousand years is called millennialism or millenarianism (from the
Latin *mille,* "a thousand") or chiliasm (from the Greek *chilioi,* "a thousand"). In general, there are three types of interpretation of this obscure
text. The first two, *postmillennialism* and *premillennialism,* take the
text literally, and the third, *amillennialism,* takes it symbolically.

Q. 94. What does postmillennialism say, and who holds it?

To some Christians the millennium represents literally a period of
a thousand years of peace that will occur once the majority of humanity
accept Jesus Christ as their Lord and Savior. As the church evangelizes
and as people convert to the Christian faith, Satan is "bound," and his
power is gradually eliminated. After one thousand years of this earthly
kingdom of God, Satan will launch a rebellion to destroy the achievements of the church. This rebellion is the Great Tribulation. It will be
brought to an end by the second coming of Christ to raise the dead,
judge the world, and usher in the new heaven and the new earth.

Because in this interpretation Christ's second coming occurs *after*
the millennium, it is called *post*millennialism. It achieved great popular-
ity in the United States from the middle of the 1700s to the beginning of
the 1800s. One of its famous champions was Jonathan Edwards
(1703–58), who through his revivalist preaching sought to awaken people to the imminent second coming. Christians of the postmillennialist
persuasion feel called to work actively to bring in the millennium by
means of missionary outreach and social reform. The "social gospel,"
which flourished at the beginning of this century with Walter Rauschen-
busch (1861–1918), was partially indebted to postmillennialism. Need-

less to say, the two world wars, along with many social and economic crises, did much to undermine the basic optimism of postmillennialism concerning the ability of the church to bring in the millennium.

Q. 95. What does premillennialism say?

Like the first theory, premillennialism takes the millennium to mean literally a period of one thousand years of Christ's reign. Differently from postmillennialism, however, premillennialism holds that Christ's second coming will occur *before* the millennium (that is why it is called *pre*millennialism). Indeed, the purpose of Christ's parousia is to establish the millennium as an actual earthly kingdom. In the premillennialist interpretation, the scenario of the end-time would be as follows: First, Christ will come back in glory. Second, he will take the Christians with him (the rapture and the first resurrection): "Blessed and holy is the one who shares in the first resurrection. The second death has no power over these; they will be priests of God and of Christ, and they will reign with him for [the] thousand years" (Rv 20:6). Third, he will defeat the antichrist and his cohort, bind Satan, and establish an earthly kingdom that lasts for a thousand years. Fourth, at the conclusion of the millennium, Satan will be allowed one last rebellion and then will be cast into the lake of fire. Fifth, Christ will raise the other dead for the judgment, followed by the formation of the new heaven and the new earth. In general, premillennialism is widespread among conservative evangelicals and fundamentalists.

Q. 96. What does amillennialism say?

Contrary to both pre- and postmillennialism, this interpretation does not take the millennium literally. In its view, there is no earthly millennium during which Christ and his faithful will rule, either before or after the second coming. That is why it is called *a*millennialism. Rather than taking Revelation as a historical description of the events of the end-time, amillennialism interprets it symbolically as describing the spiritual battles between the children of God and the powers of darkness.

One of the most influential proponents of amillennialism was Augustine (354–430). According to him, the "first resurrection" refers to the transition from death to sin to life in faith, which takes place in baptism. The "binding" of Satan refers to his defeat when the human race was redeemed by Christ. The kingdom of Christ is the church in the world. In a certain sense, Christians already share in the glorious rule of Christ, which is present in them by virtue of their baptismal victory over sin and death. This kingdom has a symbolic duration of a thousand years, one thousand being considered a perfect number. At the end of time, Christ will come again, and there will be the resurrection of the dead (the "second resurrection"), the general judgment, and eternal life.

Amillennialism is the view of the majority of Christians, including Roman Catholics, Lutherans, Presbyterians, and Southern Baptists. In my view, it is the interpretation that makes most sense, as long as the spiritualizing tendency inherent in it does not lead people to neglect their sociopolitical, cultural, and economic responsibilities that are involved in preparing for the kingdom of God.

Q. 97. Will there be a general judgment? Why should there be another judgment if we are already judged in death? Isn't the general judgment redundant?

The Creed professes that Christ will come again "to judge the living and the dead." This final judgment, of course, does not repeat the "particular judgment": we will not be subjected as it were to double jeopardy. The belief that God will judge the nations and Israel is deeply rooted in the prophets' preaching: Yahweh appears as a shepherd who sorts out the good and the bad in his flock (Ez 34:17–22), as a laborer in the harvest (Is 27:12; Jer 15:7), as treading the wine press (Is 63:1–6), and as the owner of a furnace for smelting and purifying (Ez 22:18–22). However, the "day of Yahweh" will bring not simply punishment but also salvation: God will once again look with favor upon God's people and the nations.

Of the two aspects of the divine judgment, salvation is ever more emphasized from the time of the Exile, particularly in Ezekiel and Deutero-Isaiah. In the apocalyptic literature, God's judgment assumes a preponderant place, with colorful and vivid descriptions of assortments of judicial acts, places, characters, procedures, books, scales, and forms of tortures. Their purpose, however, is not to arouse fear but to inspire confidence in those who suffer persecution for the sake of Yahweh.

In the New Testament, Jesus is portrayed as announcing the coming judgment in every phase of his ministry, for example, in the Sermon on the Mount (Mt 5:22, 26, 29; 7:1, 21, 24–27), in the discourse to the disciples (Mt 10:28, 33), in the eschatological discourse (Mk 13 and parallels), in his words to the Pharisees (Mt 23:13–25), and finally in some of the more important parables (e.g., Lk 16:1–8, 19–31; Mt 22:11 f.; 24:37 f.; 25). Jesus himself is said to be the judge in this final judgment, so that the Old Testament "day of Yahweh" becomes the "day of the Lord" (1 Cor 1:8; 1 Thes 5:2; Heb 10:25).

The general judgment serves therefore to manifest the lordship and power of Jesus. Then each of us will understand God's plan for the world and recognize the role of Jesus as well as our own within it. As the *Catechism of the Catholic Church* states, "The Last Judgment will come when Christ returns in glory....Then through his Son Jesus Christ, God will pronounce the final word on all history. We shall know the ultimate meaning of the whole work of creation and of the entire economy of salvation and understand the marvelous ways by which God's Providence led everything towards its final end" (no. 1040).

Q. 98. What are the criteria of the final judgment?

The sentence is decided by one's attitude to Jesus, which is expressed in the acceptance or refusal of his person and message and in behavior corresponding to this attitude. For Paul, the decisive criterion will be the law of faith (Rom 3:27), the "law of Christ" (1 Cor 9:21; Gal 6:2). For John, the christological criterion is decisive even during the present life: "Whoever believes in him [Jesus] will not be condemned, but whoever does not believe has already been condemned, because he has not believed in the name of the only Son of God" (Jn 3:18); "For if you do not believe that I AM, you will die in your sins" (Jn 8:24).

However, this faith in Jesus is not just an intellectual assent. It must be embodied in works: "Do not be amazed at this, because the hour is coming in which all who are in the tombs will hear his voice and will come out, those who have done good deeds to the resurrection of

life, but those who have done wicked deeds to the resurrection of condemnation" (Jn 5:28–29).

The necessity of embodying faith in love is vividly illustrated in
Jesus' discourse on the final judgment: "When the Son of Man comes in
his glory, and all the angels with him, he will sit upon his glorious
throne, and all the nations will be assembled before him....Then the
king will say to those on his right: 'Come, you who are blessed by my
Father. Inherit the kingdom prepared for you from the foundation of the
world. For I was hungry and you gave me food, I was thirsty and you
gave me drink, a stranger and you welcomed me, naked and you clothed
me, ill and you cared for me, in prison and you visited me'" (Mt
25:31–37). Here Jesus identifies himself with "these least brothers" of
his, and whatever is done for them is done for Jesus, and whatever is
denied them is denied Jesus. The ultimate criterion for the final judgment, then, is *love* for Jesus as demonstrated in love for all his brothers
and sisters, even if one is not consciously aware that one is doing the
acts of love for Jesus.

It is clear, then, that as we stand in front of the seat of divine judgment, we are brought back to earth and are asked to give an account of
what we have done with our lives to serve and love Jesus in our brothers
and sisters. Faith in the afterlife is neither an escape from our earthly
responsibilities (as Karl Marx claimed) nor a balm to rub on our emo-
tional pains (as Sigmund Freud suggested). It is, on the contrary, a spur
for us to take our earthly responsibilities with utmost seriousness.

Q. 99. Will there be a universal conflagration at the end of the world?

The only biblical text that mentions a universal fire at the end of
the world is 2 Peter 3:10–12: "But the day of the Lord will come like a
thief, and then the heavens will pass away with a mighty roar and the
elements will be dissolved by fire, and the earth and everything done on
it will be found out....the heavens will be dissolved in flames and the
elements melted by fire."

Though this is the only biblical passage about a final conflagration,
the idea was common in apocalyptic and Greco-Roman thought. Fire
stands for judgment, purification, and destruction. What 2 Peter is affirm-

ing then is that at the last judgment everyone and everything will be submitted to divine judgment; every evil and imperfection, including those found in the material universe, will be destroyed, so that "new heavens and a new earth in which righteousness dwells" (2 Pt 3:13) may appear.

Whatever interpretation one may choose to give to this statement about a final conflagration, it would be highly irresponsible to think that some kind of nuclear explosion or some world war (the Armageddon) or the destruction of the cosmos is necessary before the coming of Christ.

It would be equally irresponsible to think that because the universe will be destroyed at the end of time, we have no responsibilities toward the ecology. Such responsibilities would include, among other things, keeping the air clean, the water unpolluted, and the environment livable, both for ourselves and for future generations; using the earth's resources wisely; and respecting the intrinsic worth of all nonhuman realities. Thus, eschatological faith, rather than diminishing our ecological responsibility, intensifies it, because the universe in which we live is not just a roadside motel we stop by on our way to heaven but our permanent home. The new heaven and the new earth is not some other place, but this universe of ours transformed by the divine power.

Q. 100. What should we make of the "new heaven and new earth"?

The seer of Revelation presents us with a magnificent vision of what will happen at the end-time: "Then I saw a new heaven and a new earth. The former heaven and the former earth had passed away, and the sea was no more. I also saw the holy city, a new Jerusalem, coming down out of heaven from God, prepared as a bride adorned for her husband. I heard a loud voice from the throne saying, 'Behold, God's dwelling is with the human race. He will dwell with them and they will be his people and God himself will always be with them [as their God]. He will wipe every tear from their eyes, and there shall be no more death or mourning, wailing or pain, [for] the old order has passed away'" (Rv 21:1–4).

In all of literature there is perhaps no more eloquent expression of the deepest hopes of the human heart for happiness and perfection than these four verses. Not only will evil (the "sea") and sufferings ("tear," "death," "mourning," "wailing," and "pain") disappear forever, but there also will be an intimate communion between human beings and God ("God's dwelling is with the human race"), and the whole material universe will be included in this divine-human communion ("a new heaven and a new earth").

We would do the poetic flights of the seer terrible injustice were we to look upon his declaration as a piece of modern cosmology and astrophysics. Our scientific mind, weighed down by measurements and empirical verifications, must be lifted up by the wings of the imagination to contemplate with hopeful hearts, not what we paltry creatures can do for ourselves, but what God can and will do for us ("coming down out of heaven from God"). Then we will understand that only apocalyptic imagination and not descriptive language can get a glimpse of the final happiness God has in store for humanity and the cosmos.

Q. 101. In this new heaven and new earth, what will happen to what we have accomplished here on earth? How are this new heaven and new earth related to what we hope for our lives?

In answering the first part of this question as well as others of this type, a measure of intellectual humility, confessing ignorance, is most appropriate. As Vatican II put it, "We know neither the moment of the consummation of the earth and of humanity nor the way the universe will be transformed....When we have spread on earth the fruits of our nature and our enterprise—human dignity, brotherly communion, and freedom—according to the command of the Lord and in his Spirit, we will find them once again, cleansed this time from the stain of sin, illuminated and transfigured, when Christ presents to his Father an eternal and universal kingdom 'of truth and life, a kingdom of holiness and grace, a kingdom of justice, love and peace.' Here on earth the kingdom is mysteriously present; when the Lord comes it will enter into its perfection" (*Gaudium et Spes,* no. 39).

It is the hope of the church, then, that nothing that is true, good, and beautiful that the human community has produced will be lost; purified of their imperfections, they will find a proper and permanent place in the eternal kingdom. As to what these things may be, the only limits are those of the human imagination. At least one theologian has set his own imagination on fire and has spoken of "Halls of Science, of

Art, of Literature, Mathematics, where all man's achievements would be on record….Halls of Music…Halls of Psychology…Halls of Parapsychology…Halls of Physics…Halls of Cosmology…Halls of Philosophy…Halls of Travel, of Interplanetary Travel, of Interstellar Travel, Intergalactic Travel…" (E. J. Fortman, *Eternal Life After death,* 316). Of course, the list can go on and on.

One may chuckle at this list, which may appear as nothing more than a child's wishes on Christmas morning. And, of course, Feuerbach and Marx and Freud would be right in saying that heaven is nothing but human projection if the list is taken as a *factual description* of what the eternal kingdom is like. But what these earth-bound thinkers and their jejune imaginations fail to grasp is that this list is, not a factual description of the afterlife, but an expression of the yearning of the human heart, which is so created that it is restless until it rests in God. Without this yearning and hope, the human heart shrivels and dies, and human beings lose their dignity. In imagining these wondrous things, the human heart *hopes* that God will preserve, howsoever we do not know, all the true, the good, and the beautiful that we have achieved upon this earth because they are nothing but reflections, albeit dim and paltry, of God's own Truth, Goodness, and Beauty.

With regard to the second part of the question, we must remember that eschatology is the narrative of hope, the hope that dawned at the beginning of human history when God promised salvation to fallen humanity; the hope that took shape in God's promise to Abraham and in God's covenant with the Hebrew people; the hope that was nurtured by the prophets and apocalypticists; the hope that found fulfillment in Jesus of Nazareth; the hope that is being now sustained by the church; and the hope that will be definitively and perfectly realized in God's eternal kingdom.

Such a hope is not an idle expectation. Its flame is kept burning by faith made active in love. Whether that hope will be fulfilled for you and me personally does not depend on how much we know, not even about eschatology, or on whether we are *pre-, post-,* or *a*-millennialists. Rather, it depends on God's unfailing love for us and the depth of our response to that love by loving God's children and God's earth.

Thus, heaven brings us back to earth, to the heart of the world, where in freedom and love, and by God's pure grace, we carve out our eternal destiny.

BIBLIOGRAPHY

Note: The English translation of the Bible is taken from the New American Bible.

Aldwinckle, Russell. *Death in the Secular City: Life After Death in Contemporary Theology and Philosophy*. Grand Rapids: Eerdmans, 1972.

Barth, Karl. *The Epistle to the Romans*. London: Oxford University Press, 1933.

Becker, Ernest. *The Denial of Death*. New York: The Free Press, 1973.

Boros, Ladislaus. *The Mystery of Death*. New York: Herder and Herder, 1965.

Bregman, Lucy. *Death in the Midst of Life: Perspectives on Death from Christianity and Depth Psychology*. Grand Rapids: Baker Book House, 1992.

Catechism of the Catholic Church. New York: Paulist Press, 1994.

The Christian Faith. Edited by J. Neuner and J. Dupuis. New York: Alba House, 1982.

Collins, John J. *The Apocalyptic Imagination: An Introduction to the Jewish Matrix of Christianity*. New York: Crossroad, 1984.

Cullmann, Oscar. *Immortality of the Soul or the Resurrection of the Dead?* London: Epworth Press, 1958.

Doss, Richard. *The Last Enemy: A Christian Understanding of Death.* New York: Harper and Row, 1974.

Fortman, Edmund J. *Everlasting Life After Death.* New York: Alba House, 1976.

Habermas, Gary R., and J. P. Moreland. *Immortality: The Other Side of Death.* Nashville: Thomas Nelson Publishers, 1992.

Hayes, Zachary. *Visions of a Future: A Study of Christian Eschatology.* Collegeville: The Liturgical Press, 1989.

Hellwig, Monika. *What Are They Saying About Death and Christian Hope?* New York: Paulist Press, 1978.

International Theological Commission. "Some Current Theological Questions in Eschatology." *Irish Theological Quarterly* 58, no. 3 (1992): 209–43.

Kelly, Tony. *Touching on the Infinite: Explorations in Christian Hope.* Victoria, Australia: Collins Dove, 1991.

König, Adrio. *The Eclipse of Christ in Eschatology: Toward a Christ-Centered Approach.* Grand Rapids: Eerdmans, 1989.

Kreeft, Peter. *Everything You Ever Wanted to Know About Heaven... But Never Dreamed of Asking.* San Francisco: Ignatius Press, 1990.

Kübler-Ross, Elisabeth. *On Death and Dying.* New York: Macmillan, 1969.

Küng, Hans. *Eternal Life? Life After Death as a Medical, Philosophical, and Theological Problem.* Garden City, N.Y.: Doubleday, 1984.

Lane, Dermot. *Keeping Hope Alive.* New York: Paulist Press, 1996.

Le Goff, Jacques. *The Birth of Purgatory.* Chicago: The University of Chicago Press, 1984.

MacGregor, Geddes. *Reincarnation in Christianity.* Wheaton, Ill.: Theosophical Publishing House, 1978.

McDannell, Colleen, and Bernhard Lang. *Heaven: A History*. New York: Vintage Books, 1988.

Moody, Raymond A., Jr. *Life After Life*. Atlanta: Mockingbird Books, 1975.

Phan, Peter. "Contemporary Context and Issues in Eschatology." *Theological Studies* 55 (1994): 507–36.

———. *Culture and Eschatology: The Iconographical Vision of Paul Evdokimou*. New York: Peter Lang, 1987.

———. "Eschatology and Ecology: The Environment in the End-Time." *Dialogue & Alliance* 9, no. 2 (1995): 99–115.

———. *Eternity in Time: A Study of Karl Rahner's Eschatology*. Selinsgrove: Susquehanna University Press, 1988.

———. "Woman and the Last Things: A Feminist Eschatology." In *In the Embrace of God: Feminist Approaches to Theological Anthropology*, edited by Ann O'Hare Graff. Maryknoll, N.Y.: Orbis, 1995.

Rahner, Karl. "The Hermeneutics of Eschatological Assertions." In *Theological Investigations*. Vol. 4. Baltimore: Helicon, 1966.

———. "The Intermediate State." In *Theological Investigations*. Vol. 17. New York: Crossroad, 1981.

———. *On the Theology of Death*. New York: Herder and Herder, 1961.

———. *Our Christian Faith: Answers for the Future*. New York: Crossroad, 1981.

———. "Remarks on the Theology of Indulgences." In *Theological Investigations*. Vol. 2. Baltimore: Helicon, 1955.

Ratzinger, Joseph. *Eschatology: Death and Eternal Life*. Washington, D.C.: The Catholic University of America Press, 1988.

The Rites of the Catholic Church. New York: Pueblo Publishing Co., 1976.

Robinson, John A. T. *Jesus and His Coming*. Philadelphia: The West-minster Press, 1979.

Rose, Fr. Seraphim. *The Soul After Death*. Platina, Calif.: Saint Herman of Alaska Brotherhood, 1980.

Sachs, John R. "Apocatastasis in Patristic Theology." *Theological Studies* 54 (1993): 617–40.

———. "Current Eschatology: Universal Salvation and the Problem of Hell." *Theological Studies* 52 (1991): 227–54.

Sacred Congregation for the Doctrine of the Faith. "The Reality of Life After Death." In *Vatican Council II: More Post Conciliar Documents*, edited by Austin Flannery. Collegeville: The Liturgical Press, 1982.

Schneiders, Sandra M. *The Revelatory Text: Interpreting the New Testament as Sacred Scripture*. San Francisco: Harper San Francisco, 1991.

Thomas Aquinas, *Summa Theologiae*. New York: Benzinger Brothers, 1948.

Vatican Council II: The Conciliar and Post Conciliar Documents. Edited by Austin Flannery. Northport, N.Y.: Costello, 1975.

Von Balthasar, Hans Urs. *Dare We Hope "That All Men Be Saved"?* San Francisco: Ignatius Press, 1988.

———. *Theodramatik*. Vol. 4, Das Endspiel. Einsiedeln: Johannes Verlag, 1983.

———. *Fragen der Theologie Heute*. Einsiedeln: Benzinger Brothers, 1958.

Wainwright, Geoffrey. *Eucharist and Eschatology*. New York: Oxford University Press, 1981.

Zaleski, Carol. *Otherworld Journeys: Accounts of Near-Death Experiences in Medieval and Modern Times*. New York: Oxford University Press, 1987.